6/03

Ancient America

by
Cathryn J. Long

LUCENT BOOKS
SAN DIEGO, CALIFORNIA

THOMSON
™
GALE

Detroit • New York • San Diego • San Francisco
Boston • New Haven, Conn. • Waterville, Maine
London • Munich

On cover: Book of Ceremonies, the god
Tezcatilipoca and his retinue.

Library of Congress Cataloging-in-Publication Data

Long, Cathryn J.
    Ancient America / by Cathryn J. Long
        p.   cm.—(World history series)
Includes bibliographical references and index.
Summary: Discusses the history of ancient America, detailing
the lives of hunters and gatherers, the move toward agricul-
ture, and the rise and fall of civilizations, including the Inca,
Maya, and Aztecs.
    ISBN 1-56006-889-2 (hardback : alk. paper)
    1. Indians—Antiquities—Juvenile literature.
    2. America—Antiquities—Juvenile literature.
    I. Title. II. Series.

E58.4.L65 2002
970.013—dc21

                                                    2001006605

Contents

Foreword

Each year on the first day of school, nearly every history teacher faces the task of explaining why his or her students should study history. One logical answer to this question is that exploring what happened in our past explains how the things we often take for granted—our customs, ideas, and institutions—came to be. As statesman and historian Winston Churchill put it, "Every nation or group of nations has its own tale to tell. Knowledge of the trials and struggles is necessary to all who would comprehend the problems, perils, challenges, and opportunities which confront us today." Thus, a study of history puts modern ideas and institutions in perspective. For example, though the founders of the United States were talented and creative thinkers, they clearly did not invent the concept of democracy. Instead, they adapted some democratic ideas that had originated in ancient Greece and with which the Romans, the British, and others had experimented. An exploration of these cultures, then, reveals their very real connection to us through institutions that continue to shape our daily lives.

Another reason often given for studying history is the idea that lessons exist in the past from which contemporary societies can benefit and learn. This idea, although controversial, has always been an intriguing one for historians. Those who agree that society can benefit from the past often quote philosopher George Santayana's famous statement, "Those who cannot remember the past are condemned to repeat it." Historians who subscribe to Santayana's philosophy believe that, for example, studying the events that led up to the major world wars or other significant historical events would allow society to chart a different and more favorable course in the future.

Just as difficult as convincing students of the importance of studying history is the search for useful and interesting supplementary materials that present historical events in a context that can be easily understood. The volumes in Lucent Books' World History Series attempt to present a broad, balanced, and penetrating view of the march of history. Ancient Egypt's important wars and rulers, for example, are presented against the rich and colorful backdrop of Egyptian religious, social, and cultural developments. The series engages the reader by enhancing historical events with these cultural contexts. For example, in *Ancient Greece,* the text covers the role of women in that society. Slavery is discussed in *The Roman Empire,* as well as how slaves earned their freedom. The numerous and varied aspects of everyday life in these and other societies are explored in each volume of the series. Additionally, the series covers the major political, cultural, and philosophical ideas as the torch of civilization is passed from ancient Mesopotamia and Egypt, through Greece, Rome, Medieval Europe, and other world cultures, to the modern day.

The material in the series is formatted in a thorough, precise, and organized manner. Each volume offers the reader a comprehensive and clearly written overview of an important historical event or period. The topic under discussion is placed in a broad, historical context. For example, *The Italian Renaissance* begins with a discussion of the High Middle Ages and the loss of central control that allowed certain Italian cities to develop artistically. The book ends by looking forward to the Reformation and interpreting the societal changes that grew out of the Renaissance. Thus, students are not only involved in an historical era, but also enveloped by the events leading up to that era and the events following it.

One important and unique feature in the World History Series is the primary and secondary source quotations that richly supplement each volume. These quotes are useful in a number of ways. First, they allow students access to sources they would not normally be exposed to because of the difficulty and obscurity of the original source. The quotations range from interesting anecdotes to farsighted cultural perspectives and are drawn from historical witnesses both past and present. Second, the quotes demonstrate how and where historians themselves derive their information on the past as they strive to reach a consensus on historical events. Lastly, all of the quotes are footnoted, familiarizing students with the citation process and allowing them to verify quotes and/or look up the original source if the quote piques their interest.

Finally, the books in the World History Series provide a detailed launching point for further research. Each book contains a bibliography specifically geared toward student research. A second, annotated bibliography introduces students to all the sources the author consulted when compiling the book. A chronology of important dates gives students an overview, at a glance, of the topic covered. Where applicable, a glossary of terms is included.

In short, the series is designed not only to acquaint readers with the basics of history, but also to make them aware that their lives are a part of an ongoing human saga. Perhaps then they will come to the same realization as famed historian Arnold Toynbee. In his monumental work, *A Study of History,* he wrote about becoming aware of history flowing through him in a mighty current, and of his own life "welling like a wave in the flow of this vast tide."

IMPORTANT DATES IN THE HISTORY OF ANCIENT AMERICA

30,000 B.C.–12,000 B.C.
First people arrive in North America from Asia.

4000
People of the Amazon basin first grow manioc.

7000
Agriculture begins in the Andes and in Mesoamerica.

2500
Growing corn becomes common throughout Mesoamerica.

2000–1000
Squash and other plants become domesticated in the eastern woodlands of North America.

1000
Bow and arrow first appear in the Americas and spread throughout the continents by A.D. 1500.

460
The religious center of Chavin de Huantar begins to develop in the Andes.

250–900
Classic Maya civilization reaches its peak.

30,000 B.C.	4000	3500	2000	1500	1000	500	A.D. 1

5500–2000
First American pottery is created in the Amazon basin.

2000
First monument ceremonial centers are built in the Andes region.

500
The city of Monte Alban is founded in Mexico's Oaxaca Valley. Some of the oldest writing of the Americas is carved in stone at Monte Alban.

3500
First cotton is harvested along the west coast of South America.

A.D. 1
Complex chiefdoms based on fishing and agriculture begin to form in the Amazon basin.

9000
People are present at the southern tip of South America.

1500–600
The Olmec culture flourishes along the coast of the Gulf of Mexico.

1–800
Moche civilization dominates the north coast of the Andes region.

600
City of Teotihuacan,
Valley of Mexico
reaches its height.

1350
Aztec civilization
begins to form.

1534
Jacques Cartier
claims Canadian
region for France.

1000
Corn and beans
begin to be culti-
vated throughout
North America.

1533
Pizarro subdues
the Inca empire.

1621
Thanksgiving
celebration is
attended by
natives and
British settlers
at Plymouth.

1494
Treaty of Tordesillas
divides the Americas
between Spain and
Portugal.

1100–1300
Ancestral Pueblans
build their most
spectacular villages
of conjoined houses
at Mesa Verde in
southwest North
America.

1438
Pachakuti founds
the Inca empire.

500	1000	1100	1200	1300	1400	1500	1600

1115
Chaco Canyon Great
Houses and turquoise
trade reach their peak in
southwest North America.

1492
Christopher
Columbus arrives
on the island
of Hispaniola.

1050–1250
City of Cahokia, the
largest in North America
at that time, prospers on
the Mississippi River.

1584
Britain
claims all
of North
America
not inhabited
by Christians.

1519
Cortés begins
to conquer the
Aztecs.

650
City of Tiwanaku
and its domain in
the central Andes
region achieves
its peak.

1428
Aztec empire is created
with the formation of the
Triple Alliance.

1530s
Capitania system
begins in Brazil.

The Nature of Ancient American History

The history of America before the arrival of Europeans almost went untold—yet every year, more of it is revealed.

The first human beings who arrived in America were part of a wave of people which slowly spread from Africa to other continents. Some of these people first migrated to Europe and Asia about one hundred thousand years ago. In time, a few groups of people reached the Pacific Ocean, and even crossed the water to Australia. Eventually, fourteen thousand years ago or earlier, human groups began to cross from Asia to the Americas.

These groups, like people everywhere at the time, had survival skills and tools of stone, bone, and wood. Equally important, they had a culture which bound them in groups and explained their place in the world. But they did not yet practice agri-

Ancient American cultures ranged from nomadic hunter-gatherers to complex civilizations such as the Maya, who built impressive cities like Chichén Itzá (pictured) in Mexico.

A CREATION STORY

Traditional native history includes creation stories such as this one from the Okanagan people of the North American northwest. This version, told by Ella Clark and adapted by Richard Erdoes, appears in The Telling of the World: Native American Stories and Art, *edited by W.S. Penn.*

"The earth was once a human being: Old One made her out of a woman. 'You will be the mother of all people,' he said.

Earth is alive yet, but she has been changed. The soil is her flesh, the rocks are her bones, the wind is her breath, trees and grass are her hair. She lives spread out, and we live on her. . . .

After taking the woman and changing her to earth, Old One gathered some of her flesh and rolled it into balls, as people do with mud or clay. He made the first group of these balls into the ancients, the beings of the early world. . . . Old One made the people out of the last balls of mud he took from the earth. He rolled them over and over, shaped them like Indians, and blew on them to bring them alive. . . . Old One made people and animals into males and females that they might breed and multiply. Thus all living things came from the earth. When we look around, we see part of our mother everywhere."

culture or the complex way of life known today as civilization. During the thousands of years before European explorers arrived in 1492, the people now called native Americans or American Indians developed in near-total isolation from the rest of the world.

The isolation of the Native Americans did not mean that they all remained the same. An enormous variety of societies arose. Groups progressed at their own rates, developed their own special qualities, and sometimes disappeared. Three basic kinds of social and cultural organization can be traced: hunter-gatherer bands, agricultural villagers, and complex civilizations. All these societies developed in the Americas, but not always in that sequence. For example, in what is now Louisiana, mobile hunter-gatherers called the Poverty Point people built enormous structures, as sophisticated as those of the better-known Inca. Inhabitants of great cities, like the Maya of Cerros, eventually abandoned their elaborate urban centers and returned to agricultural villages. When the Europeans arrived, they found natives living in a huge variety of ways, often quite close to one another. The rich and settled people of the North

American northwest coast, for example, lived in decorated wooden houses, hosted elegant social events, and dressed in finely made robes. Yet the inland neighbors with whom they traded were hunter-gatherers, much like their earliest ancestors. They wore and owned little as they searched for food in the wilderness.

The various peoples of the Americas developed their own forms of history, just as the Europeans did. Every group had its own creation story, a story that connected the people to their part of the earth and helped explain their role in it. Elders were keepers of memory in all native societies. With stories, songs, poetry, and ritual, they kept alive the traditions and events of the past most meaningful to them. Objects, too, embodied history. A pipe could remind a smoker of the ancestor who made it. Smoking that pipe honored the spirit of the ancestor.

Native Americans regularly associated history with spiritual meaning. This connection could be simple, as in the smoking of an ancestral pipe, or very complex. The Maya of Central America, for instance, surrounded some of their buildings with upright stone slabs, called stelae. Each stela was engraved with pictures and writing containing the history of the past rulers. Yet the engravings also refer to gods and supernatural events. To the Maya, as to all native Americans, a host of powers and spirits shared the same stage as human history.

HISTORY LOST—AND REGAINED

One terrible effect of the European arrival was to deny the importance or even the existence of the natives' long and colorful history. Because the traditions of the Americas were so different from those of Europe, it was nearly impossible for the Europeans to recognize that these people had a history, or a valid way of recording it. Native records, where they existed in objects, writing, or pictures, were often destroyed by the Europeans because they did not suit European religious or scholarly ideas. History, passed on to the young by their elders, faded when disease, war, and forced removal interrupted normal child raising and tribal ceremonies. Within a few generations of the arrival of Europeans, therefore, much of the history of ancient America was lost.

That harsh fact is not the end of the story, though. Despite the destruction of their past, native people have managed to keep their history alive in many ways. It exists in place names, songs, family stories, myths, and rituals. It also endures in ancient American buildings, earthen monuments, and carvings and paintings on

A carving from La Venta, Mexico, shows a king in full regalia.

rocks or in caves. Ancient American history lives on in very old objects, preserved privately or in museums. Today, more native memories are being written down and incorporated into broader historical accounts.

Modern historians are attempting to include native memories with other forms of evidence about the past. One source of information is the study of traditional cultures living today. Sometimes this process is called "backstreaming," because it suggests following a stream to its source. An example is the study of kin groups in modern Peru called *ayllus*. It is likely that some aspects of *ayllu* organization today are the same as they were when the *ayllu* system supported the Inca civilization. Of course, historians must be very careful in using this approach, for there can be many reasons for differences between past and present peoples.

Another source of evidence, also needing careful study, is writing and pictures produced by the first Europeans to encounter native people. As valuable as such accounts can be, they also are biased, not only by the prejudices of the writers, but also by the fact that Europeans usually saw only limited aspects of native life.

A Bolivian archaeologist studies a carved stone block from a pre-Inca site.

CONTRIBUTIONS FROM ARCHAEOLOGY AND TECHNOLOGY

The greatest contributor to current knowledge about ancient America is archaeology: the science of finding and learning from ancient evidence buried in the earth. Archaeology did not begin in the Americas until the mid–nineteenth century, when archaeologists began to rediscover grand sites such as the Maya cities and the mound complexes of North America. Archaeological finds helped the world realize that the Americas had a fascinating history worthy of respect. Many gaps remain in what archaeologists know about ancient America. Yet every year, new knowledge comes to light.

Technology also has triggered many new discoveries. Recently, for instance, scholars have used electron microscopy and computer anlysis to detect the fur and fiber origins of ancient textiles. Locating building sites underground has become easier due to magnetometry, a means of electronically picturing what is under the ground. These fresh discoveries continue to revise the written history of events and peoples in the Americas before 1492. In an exciting way, America's ancient history lost after European contact is today being recovered by a new flow of knowledge.

1 Hunters and Gatherers

The story of ancient America extends from the arrival of the first people more than fourteen thousand years ago to the shock of European contact only five hundred years ago. For thousands of years, the people of the American continents lived in near isolation from the rest of the world, developing their own varied societies. Those societies felt a close connection between themselves and the natural environment, a connection created and reinforced by a long tradition of hunting and gathering.

Hunting and gathering means living off the natural land: hunting game, catching fish, and foraging for edible plants and insects. Like other human beings around the world, all native Americans were hunters and gatherers until about eight thousand years ago. Then, the beginning of agriculture allowed many native people to settle in permanent villages. Later, civilizations flourished in parts of the Americas. Yet hunting and gathering never died out, as it did in much of Europe and Asia with the rise of farming and cities. Instead, some American groups remained hunter-gatherers through the time of European contact and beyond. Many others did some farming, but continued to hunt and gather also. Even full-time farmers and city dwellers kept customs, beliefs, and views of the world first established by their hunter-gatherer ancestors.

THE FIRST HUNTER-GATHERERS

The first people to inhabit the American continents were hunter-gatherers from northern Asia. They probably arrived between twenty thousand and fourteen thousand years ago, near the end of the last Ice Age, when low sea levels revealed a wide piece of land called Beringia between northeast Asia and what is now Alaska. Asian bands crossed on foot or skirted the land by canoe to arrive in North America. From there, they moved southward, reaching the tip of South America at least eleven thousand years ago. As the Ice Age ended, the seas rose again and Beringia was covered by water. This event closed the door on migrating people almost entirely, for few would brave the dangers and mysteries of the open sea. Those who had already arrived were the ancestors of the people now called native Americans.

The first American arrivals were used to a wandering life in the harsh environment of the Ice Age. As in Asia, glaciers, slow-moving mountains of ice miles thick, covered much of the northern land and extended over the mountain ranges. Where there were no glaciers, the land was generally tundra or grassland, with small open forests. Feeding on the grassy plains—and sometimes on each other—were huge Ice Age mammals such as the

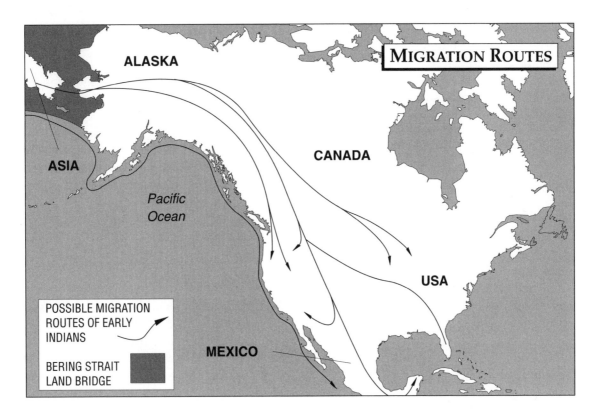

ALASKA

ASIA

Pacific
Ocean

CANADA

USA

MEXICO

POSSIBLE MIGRATION
ROUTES OF EARLY
INDIANS

BERING STRAIT
LAND BRIDGE

elephant-like mastodon and the saber-toothed tiger.

Among the bones of these ancient animals, archaeologists have found human-made stone points. The points were carefully chipped to razor sharpness, then mounted on wood or bone handles to form knives and spears. These very old stone points prove the importance of hunting to the earliest Americans. In fact, camps and "kill" sites which resemble one another through many centuries suggest that the hunting methods of the first arrivals and their descendants changed little during the Ice Age. Many of these people, called Paleo-Indians, seem to have been swift-moving hunters who followed migrating herds of large animals. Only a small amount of evidence indicates these peoples' use of plants, possibly

These spear points from Wyoming are about 10,000 years old.

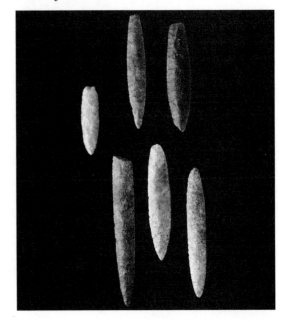

because plant materials are perishable. At Monte Verde in what is now Chile, however, archaeologist Tom D. Dillehay found plant remains preserved by a bog. He says this evidence shows some Paleo-Indians lived mostly on wild potatoes and "[a] wide variety of edible seeds, stalks, leaves, fruits, nuts, berries, and roots."[1]

Paleo-Indians generally lived in small bands of fewer than two dozen people, but sometimes met in large, multiband gatherings. They were skilled in making coiled and twined basketry. Their hunting tools included the spear-thrower, or atlatl, and various snares designed to trap small animals. They used eyed needles to sew clothing, including moccasin-style footwear. Inside caves, some of them drew animals, made handprints, and ate wild seeds—including some which caused visions. Some or all of these practices may have originated in Asia; all survived into later times.

These hints of Paleo-Indian life are intriguing, but the evidence remains so sparse that it is difficult to draw reliable conclusions about their life ways. For example, the presence of mind-altering seeds may mean the seeds were used in religious events, as they were thousands of years later. But there is no way to know yet if the religious practices had developed. There is much more reliable evidence to suggest how the people lived after the Ice Age came to an end.

THE ICE AGE ENDS

The earth slowly warmed as the Ice Age ended, about ten thousand years ago. The glaciers retreated northward or to the tops of mountains, grasslands shrank, and vast areas of open pine forest and tundra were covered with hardwood forest or, in the tropics, with rain forest. Old waterways

The gigantic Ice Age mammals such as the woolly mammoth (pictured) died out around 10,000 years ago.

TRACKING DOWN THE PALEO-INDIANS

In her book, In Search of Ancient America, *writer Heather Pringle describes how Canadian archaeologist Jacques Cinq-Mars found clear evidence that people were in the far north over twenty thousand years ago.*

"In 1983 while working in the laboratory sorting through bone scraps, he came across something hauntingly familiar: a large talon-shaped [bone] flake tool almost identical to those excavated a decade earlier along the Old Crow River [in the extreme Canadian northwest]. Encouraged, he returned to Bluefish [a site along the Crow] a few months later with a small team of French colleagues. And as they labored quietly, someone called him over. Just above bedrock lay a foot-long chunk of mammoth bone scarred by percussive blows. 'And right then and there it clicked,' says Cinq-Mars. 'The shape of the scar on that bone reminded me of the flake I'd picked up the winter before in the lab.' Bundling the precious bone in his hand luggage, Cinq-Mars carted it back to Ottawa himself. Hurrying into the laboratory, he dug out the talon-shaped flake from the drawers and held it up to the scar. 'It was a perfect match.'

Team members reveled in the news. Unearthed from a high ridgetop cave, the flake tool could not have been splintered by river ice nor shattered by trampling animals around a waterhole. Nor did it reveal any gouging or scraping marks from carnivores' sharp teeth. Instead, a Beringian hunter had clearly struck it off from the mammoth bone core in a series of deliberate, sequential steps. The burning question was when. . . .

When the final set of dates rolled in . . . the mammoth-bone flake and core dated back some 23,500 years—to the bitterest cold of the last glaciation."

disappeared or changed, and the rivers and lakes of today formed. In the course of these changes, the large Ice Age mammals became extinct, certain plants died out, and other animals and plants took their place. The changes were gradual, but tremendous, and had a great impact on the people. Bands of hunter-gatherers spread out into every environmental niche, coming to know intimately the changed land and its creatures.

Archaeologist Thomas F. Lynch speaks of America after the end of the Ice Age as "a vast laboratory in which hunter-gatherer cultures conducted careful experiments in adaptation"[2] for the next five thousand years. Although change continued even after that, the process of settling in after the Ice Age led to patterns of life that persisted for generations.

BANDS, TRIBES, AND TERRITORIES

The mobile band as a basic social unit was one thing that did not change at the end of the Ice Age. Just as was probably true in Paleo-Indian times, bands consisted of related families. Blood ties reinforced ties of friendship and practical dependence on one another. Most American Indians kept careful track of their kinfolk. Some bands were the same as clans, which were groups of relatives who were not considered eligible to marry one another. Other bands included more than one clan, but the need to "marry out," to find a partner who was not part of the family group, encouraged bands to get together from time to time.

After the Ice Age, bands did not travel as widely as they had before. Instead, most bands remained within a roughly defined territory which they occupied with other bands who spoke the same language and shared the same heritage. The term "tribe" is often used to describe such a group of bands (though this sense is different from what is meant by a modern American Indian tribe). Many ancient tribes had no formal political organiza-tion or chiefs. They simply thought of themselves as "the people."

Language can be used to estimate the number of tribes. The earliest Americans probably spoke a variety of languages. When bands settled into territories, these languages slowly changed in isolation from one another, and even greater variety evolved. At the time of European contact, one to two thousand languages were spoken, corresponding to the same number of tribes. At least three hundred of those were North American, and the rest were South American. Probably there were more small tribes in South America, because these groups were more isolated from each other by geographical barriers such as high mountains and thick jungles.

Within their territories, most bands moved from place to place to take maximum advantage of the available resources. Seasonal change was one trigger to movement. In the North American northeast, for example, bands of Algonquin moved inland from the shore each winter to hunt along the rivers. In spring, they moved back eastward again, to collect plants in the coastal area and to feast on shellfish at the shore. Bands in the nearly seasonless South American rain forest moved often because there was no large seasonal bounty (such as autumn nuts). In order to get enough to eat, people had to find a great variety of food. Anthropologist David J. Wilson explains the foods sought by a surviving tribe of rain forest hunter-gatherers:

> Nukak subsistence is based on the hunting and collecting of a variety of animal and plant species as well as other wild resources, such as honey. Among the frequently hunted animals

THE SALMON SETTLERS

In a few cases, hunter-gatherers lived amid so much bounty that they did not need to move. One example is the cultures of the North American northwest, where abundant sea- and land-based life allowed the people to build permanent plank houses, develop elaborate arts, and create social ranks based on wealth. At the heart of that society was the chief game animal, the salmon. Archaeologist Brian M. Fagan quotes this native prayer to the salmon in his book, Kingdoms of Gold, Kingdoms of Jade.

We have come to meet alive, Swimmer,
   do not feel wrong about what I have done
     to you,
   friend Swimmer,
   for that is the reason why you came,
   that I may spear you,
   that I may eat you,
   Supernatural one, you, Long-Life-Giver,
     you, Swimmer.
   Now protect me and my wife.

are five species of monkey as well as the white-lipped peccary [a kind of wild pig], the land tortoise . . . and birds. . . . Insect foods include the . . . palm grub. . . . A variety of useful plant species is found here as well, many . . . unknown, except to botanists, in the outside world. These species include plants that are used as sources of . . . fish poison, and . . . the poison used on blowgun darts to stun monkeys and other small game; several types of palms; and many fruit-bearing trees.[3]

To find such food, the Nukak must be extremely attentive to the natural environment. Hunter-gatherers become accustomed to noticing cues to plant and animal life, such as the look of a leaf, the smell of the breeze, or the softest sound. When the hunting and gathering was done in the same territory generation after generation, the people became still closer to their specific natural world, memorizing its features and fitting their lives to its pattern of resources.

A MINIMUM OF POSSESSIONS

Hunter-gatherers had to make the most of their environment with a minimum of objects that might make life easier or more pleasant. When Europeans encountered natives with almost no possessions, they concluded that the people were inferior. However, baggage is a hardship to a people who must move often. There were no wheeled carts in the Americas,

GUESSING GAMES

Janet Berlo tells about musical guessing games which help sharpen powers of observation and memory needed by hunter-gatherers. This passage is from a chapter on "Arts" from Native America: Portrait of the Peoples, *edited by Duane Champagne.*

"The most popular games are handgames and stickgames. As social and sometimes religious activities, these guessing games are found almost everywhere in North America. Ordinarily, the players sing while hiding an object or the mark on a stick. Their opponents guess the location of the hidden object or mark, and then it is their turn to sing and hide. Each team scores points for fooling its competitors, and the first team to reach a specified point total wins the stakes. Each team has lucky songs and experienced guessers, and the game cannot exist without the music.

Ordinarily, the melodies are simple and easy to sing, with short, repeated phrases, so that the players can concentrate on winning the game. Among the Northwest Coast and northern California tribes (such as the Tolowa), stickgame songs have complicated rhythms and often contain multipart singing. In the Great Basin . . . and Central California . . . men and women play entirely separate games and have gender-specific songs. Instrumental accompaniment is supplied by drums, sticks, rattles, or clapping sticks."

probably because there were no animals capable of pulling them. Dogs, which may have accompanied the first hunters to arrive from Asia, did drag some burdens. In South America, llamas were eventually raised to carry packs. Most people, however, had to manage with what they themselves could carry. They therefore depended heavily on their intimate knowledge of their environmnet and skills to find and fashion materials into whatever was needed on the spot.

Clever technology had an important role in the few possessions of hunter-gatherers. The netted hammock, for instance, weighed little, folded up small, yet provided a comfortable, breezy bed off the ground in the tropics. A small bit of bear grease in a leather pouch served to flavor food, keep insects away, and dress the hair. Some technological innovations spread widely among hunter-gatherers and improved their quality of life. One was the toggle harpoon point,

Spears with their original shafts and bindings, created in Utah between A.D. 700 and 1200.

which caught in the flesh of prey and allowed hunters to capture sea mammals efficiently. The toggle point spread rapidly all across the arctic edge of North America after 700 B.C. Another innovation was the bow and arrow, which arrived in North America (probably from Asia) about 1000 B.C. By A.D. 1500, the weapon was known and made by virtually every group in the Americas.

For the most part, though, hunter-gatherer bands tended to make and use objects in traditional ways. It was quickest and easiest to build a house, make a spear, or weave a basket as the elders had done it before—especially if the house had to be built anew every few days or weeks, and the few tools that could be carried wore out quickly.

Efficient workmanship also meant that little time was spent decorating objects. Exceptions to this rule normally were objects with special, often spiritual, significance to the group. For example, among the Blackfeet of the Rocky Mountains, a "medicine bundle" including a sacred pipe, tobacco, and herbs was kept wrapped in the carefully cured skins of many different animals. Special significance indicated by decoration could extend to the body itself. Tattooing and body painting were common all over ancient America, as were jewelry and pierced body ornaments. Among tribes going to war in the North American southeast, for instance, the color red in paint, feathers, and other decorations reflected the appropriate state of mind.

ROLES WITHIN THE BAND

The efficiency hunter-gatherers needed to find food and take care of their other needs was largely provided by traditional roles within the band. One of the most important traditions, probably brought from Asia, made men the hunters and women the gatherers. It followed that men made the tools of hunting, and women made the tools and containers needed for gathering. In some places, these labor

These graceful ivory spear points were made 1500 years ago by the Inuit.

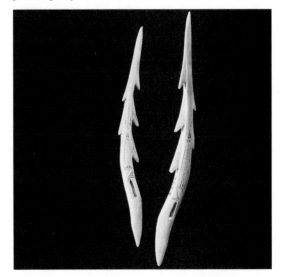

THE ATLATL

The atlatl, or spear-thrower, probably came with the earliest people to the Americas and remained in use into recent times. In The Atlatl in North America, *James H. Kellar explains how the tool is used and the extraordinary power it gives to a spear or dart.*

"The atlatl is basically a device which adds length to the user's arm. . . . The essential device is little more than a stick with provisions supplied on one end for grasping and a . . . projection on the other to engage a nock or conical depression on the [back] end of a spear. These two elements [atlatl and spear] are held in the thrower's hand . . . the long axis of both being approximately parallel. The spear is steadied with the aid of the fingers and sometimes rests on the knuckles. Motion is imparted by an overhand throwing movement. A sharp snap of the wrist at the moment of release initiates the independent flight of the dart. The spearthrower remains in the hand of the user.

. . . Its purely utilitarian usage in hunting and warfare was also enlarged to the point where it became a highly significant symbol of rank and authority. . . . [Experts] indicate that the extreme range was in the vicinity of three hundred feet. . . .

Nelson [an authority on Eskimo culture] says, 'The Eskimo are very expert in casting spears with the throwing stick. The small, light spears used in hunting seals are cast from 30 to 50 yards with considerable accuracy and force. I have seen them practice by the hour throwing a spear at waterfowl, and their accuracy is remarkable.'

[The atlatl] was the most feared device encountered by the Spanish in Peru. The high velocity of the thrown projectile coupled with its weight was sufficient to penetrate the armor of the foreign army and inflict deep and severe wounds."

divisions extended further: women and men had other exclusive duties and possessions. However, in case of need or emergency, it was common for hunter-gatherers to bend the rules for the good of the group. For instance, as one observer noted, the Ona women of South America occasionally had to hunt when the men were away. They brought home meat—although "in these cases the dogs did most of the work, including the kill, since the women never used any of the Ona weapons."[4]

Whatever their role, hunter-gatherers knew that the good of the group had to come first, since they depended on one another for life itself. The chief was expected to show this virtue most clearly. One religious historian explains,

> Selflessness and unvarying attention to others' needs . . . were the hallmarks of "chiefly" status. . . . Hunting and gathering peoples . . . reveal the religious and cultural challenges all Native American peoples have always faced. They lived in hostile environments peopled by beings who could injure, maim, and kill as easily as they could sustain life. Loners could not survive.[5]

Of course, leaders often fell short of the selfless "chiefly" ideal; but the goal remained the collective good, rather than the good of the individual. The choice of leaders also honored skills and knowledge —not possessions or inherited position. Leaders were usually chosen informally and had limited authority. They were expected to gain the advice and consent of others in the group.

Sometimes leaders themselves, the elders were always important advisers to the leaders. In addition, a vital part of their role was to teach the young. This instruction was generally an informal process, but traditional stories and ceremonies helped the elders transmit knowledge and values intact from generation to generation. The refrain of a song or story or the

This shell, carved in Georgia around A.D. 1000, depicts a flying shaman.

steps of a dance could aid memory and perpetuate the same information over many hundreds of years.

A final important role was that of the shaman, a religious expert and healer. The origins of shamanism are not clear, although it is likely that shamans, male and female, existed among the earliest Paleo-Indians. A band might have had several shamans or depended on one in a neighboring band. An important part of the shaman's role was to know and find plants which could aid the band, medically and spiritually. Shamans regularly used plants with healing properties. Many of them also used hallucinogens, mind-altering plants, as a way to travel to spiritual realms. Using plants, special objects, and rituals, the shaman worked to heal the sick or wounded, to increase the band's fortune in hunting or gathering, to send the dead away safely, and above all to honor the forces and spirits thought to have the greatest power in the world.

NATURE AND SPIRITS

Native Americans recognized supernatural forces and spirits as part of the natural world they moved through. For hunters, animals were especially important figures. Mircea Eliade writes that traditional hunters "regard animals as similar to human beings but endowed with supernatural powers; they believe that a man can change into an animal and vice versa; that the souls of the dead can enter animals; finally, that mysterious relations exist between a certain person and a certain animal."[6] Some of the most spiritually powerful beings were the most physically dangerous, including bears, panthers, and poisonous snakes in North America, and southward from Mexico jaguars, crocodiles, and serpents. It was believed that an animal could befriend a person, and many tribes regarded certain animals as their relatives or ancestors. Names of clans in North America such as Turtle, Wolf, and Deer express that relation.

Not only animals, but also plants and even natural features were thought to possess life, will, and various powers. Human beings were supposed to fit into this natural and spiritual world. Rituals and prayers were performed to balance human needs and the bounty of food from animals and plants. Keeping the balance could include an act of sacrifice: giving up something of value in return for continued well-being. This act could take a variety of forms, such as throwing a piece of meat into the fire or abstaining from sex.

Many groups thought human rituals helped keep the entire natural world in order. The Navajo, for example, according to religious historian Kenneth Morrison, "have continued to create in their tradi-

A Zapotec ceramic urn in the shape of a man wearing a jaguar headdress.

tional ceremonies that exquisite balance in the world they call *hoz'ho,* a term that expresses beauty, harmony, knowledge, and well-being." The other side of the coin, however, is that human actions also could cause imbalance in the world. "Disaster," Morrison says, "whether personal, social, military, or ecological, may therefore be the result of the people's failings."[7]

For many tribes, the activities of the spirits took place not only in the visible world, but also above in a realm of the sky, and below in a watery underworld. Some shamans were thought to be able to fly among these levels in order to meet and interact with other spirits. Many North and South American stories and ceremonies focus on the idea of a central tree or vertical axis that connects those worlds and represents the levels of existence.

CEREMONIES

Such concepts about the true nature of the world were recalled and enacted in ceremonies. Bands normally assembled with other bands a few times a year for this purpose. They were planned to mark important matters such as the renewal of the seasons or the bounty of the hunt. Ceremonies usually combined traditional dances, music, storytelling, and feasting.

To the participants, dancing, describing, and enacting these events actually helped make them happen. People thus participated in the natural unfolding of events. The same idea, that human actions helped cause natural events, lay behind ceremonies which marked key times in the life of a tribe, such as initiation of children into adulthood or the journey of those who had died to a spirit realm.

Because they brought bands together, ceremonies were also times for leaders to reach new agreements and for families to arrange marriages. People had a chance to relax for a few days, eat together, and

THE PLACE OF HUMAN BEINGS

To most native people of the Americas, human beings are only one kind of creature among many on the earth. This Skagit story from the Pacific Northwest shows animals helping the Creator arrange a world in which "human beings would have to keep out of their way." It appears in The Telling of the World: Native American Stories and Art, *edited by W.S. Penn.*

"In the beginning, Raven and Mink and Coyote helped the Creator plan the world. They were in on all the arguments. They helped the Creator decide to have all the rivers flow only one way; they first thought that the water should flow up one side of the river and down the other. They decided that there should be bends in the rivers, so that there would be eddies where the fish could stop and rest. They decided that beasts should be placed in the forests. Human beings would have to keep out of their way.

Human beings will not live on this earth forever, agreed Raven and Mink, Coyote, and Old Creator. They will stay only for a short time. Then the body will go back to the earth and the spirit back to the spirit world. All living things, they said, will be male and female—animals and plants, fish and birds. And everything will get its food from the earth, the soil."

exchange ideas and goods. These exchanges could also happen when an unusual event brought bands together —such as the ripening of an extraordinary amount of fruit or the arrival of visitors or traders.

TRADE AND WAR

Archaeological evidence shows that some items changed hands as soon as there were enough people to form links from place to place. Shell from the continental coasts made its way inland. Useful and beautiful stones such as transparent quartz and black obsidian were also spread far from their points of origin. However, it is not clear that these movements were all due to what we now call trade.

This thousand-year-old copper face most likely depicts a warrior.

Interactions between strangers or near-strangers usually took place on many levels. A trader might also be a political emissary hoping to resolve a dispute, and possibly a social emissary seeking wives or husbands for his people. Often, a natural suspicion or hostility had to be overcome. The exchange of gifts made hostility less likely by creating a bond of obligation on each side. Rituals, such as the sharing of a calumet pipe in North America, also helped strangers get along. A French priest in Canada noted the multifaceted nature of native trade in 1724: "The Indian tribes have traded with each other from time immemorial. . . . The feasts and dances which they have when they go to deal with other tribes make their trade an agreeable diversion. . . . Their ways of engaging in trade is by an exchange of gifts."[8]

Sometimes, however, friendly interactions were not possible. Aggravations were often handled by raiding another band for property, prisoners, even heads or scalps. Men planned for raids on the enemy as they prepared for important hunting expeditions, lining up spiritual help as best they could through ritual, prayer, and certain body decoration and procedures. A great warrior, like a great hunter, was a respected figure. Warfare could be devastating, though, when one group threatened to take over the territory of another. Bands were sometimes eliminated or displaced by war.

Changes even greater than those brought by warfare occurred when hunter-gatherer bands began to settle permanently. Around the world, agriculture has been acknowledged as the chief factor that allowed settlement and the cultural complexity which followed.

Chapter

2 The Practice and Impact of Agriculture

Agriculture means cultivating the land: growing crops and raising livestock useful to humans. The practice of agriculture began in the Americas, as it did all over the world, between seven thousand and nine thousand years ago. The American version of farming, though, gave special emphasis to plants. Over thousands of years, the natives collected, manipulated, and grew plants for food, medicine, and spiritual uses. They gained what archaeologist Brian M. Fagan calls "a brilliant expertise with all kinds of native plants" which lay at the essence of their culture. By 1492, native Americans had bred special forms of at least three hundred species—many more domesticated species than were developed by any society elsewhere in the world at the time. "They were, without question," Fagan says, "the world's greatest plant breeders of the day."[9]

The accomplishments of ancient American agriculture certainly began with the attentiveness of hunter-gatherer bands to the wealth of living things around them. As the processes of agriculture developed, more and more groups became agriculturalists—some only partially, some completely. Wherever agriculture was intensively practiced, it influenced the behavior and the mindset of the community, allowing new social organization on a large scale.

AGRICULTURE BEGINS

The expertise Fagan describes developed in stages and varied in its timing and location within the continents. In general, three stages mark the movement toward full agriculture. First, wild plants are tended where they grow. Second, plants or their seeds are transplanted to more fertile or convenient places. Third, people select the best plants and develop improved varieties through selective growing. This last process is called plant domestication.

Natives in various parts of the Americas discovered agricultural processes independently of each other. The plants that were grown varied with the region. In the eastern woodlands of North America, for instance, which stretched from the Mississippi to the East Coast, a group of plants called the "Eastern Agricultural Complex" was domesticated after 3000 B.C. The plants in the complex included sunflowers, goosefoot, squash, sumpweed, erect knotweed, maygrass, and little barley. Another place where agriculture seems to have begun independently is the tropical lowlands of the Amazon. There, beginning after 4000 B.C., people cultivated sweet or bitter manioc for its large roots.

A supply of manioc or other crops made it easier for people to stay longer in one place, as there was less need for hunting and gathering wild foods. More

THE PRACTICE AND IMPACT OF AGRICULTURE ■ 25

permanent settlement led in time to full-blown civilizations in two areas: the valleys of the Andes and Mesoamerica, a cultural region which stretches from what is now southern Mexico to Costa Rica.

DIGGING UP THE POTATO

The early beginnings of agriculture in the Andes, between 7000 and 8000 B.C., may have resulted from the region's geography. Valleys at different elevations provided a great variety of microenvironments: places where different kinds of plants can thrive with the right temperature, rainfall, and soil. Very early in ancient times, people moved among these valleys to gather the variety of foods they offered. Probably, these people soon found that certain plants could do well far from their wild areas of origin. And some plants could be selected and bred for certain growing conditions.

The potato, originally a high-elevation wild plant, was one of those bred to suit a wider spectrum of environments. By the time Europeans arrived in the mid-1500s, the Andeans were growing more than three thousand varieties of potato. In fact, it is likely that an interrelated set of plants and animals were domesticated at the same time in the Andes: the potato, along with a grain called quinoa, and the alpaca, llama, and guinea pig.

The Andes were home to wild camelids, ancestors of today's llama and alpaca. (Some wild camelids exist in South

SLASH-AND-BURN FARMING

To open space so the sun could reach their crops, and to fertilize the soil, native people would "slash and burn" the forest. Louis C. Faron describes the process in the Amazonian tropical forest in America in 1492, *edited by Alvin M. Josephy Jr.*

"Designating an area for clearing, the head of the household strode about . . . and directed the others to girdle the large trees with their stone axes [cut a deep ring in their trunks], slashing the bark deeply enough so that the generative sap would not rise. The huge trees would soon shed their leaves, allowing sunlight to reach down to the forest floor. Smaller trees were cut down and burned, along with the brush undercover. The ashes contained potash fertilizer that had a soil-restorative effect but which, nevertheless, leached out rather easily when the rains came. Soil depletion, plus the rapid takeover of weeds, necessitated the abandonment of fields after a few years, and cultivation would shift to another area. The cycle was repeated over and over."

A llama at the ancient Inca city of Machu Picchu in the Andes Mountains. Llamas have been used as beasts of burden in the Andes for over 8,000 years.

America today.) Watchful hunters probably noted long ago that these creatures had a strong herd instinct and "pecking order," which meant they would follow leaders easily. People could therefore slip in at the top of that order to direct a herd. Captured animals were kept and bred in rock corrals. One theory holds that abandoned corrals acted as excellent garden areas for domesticated plants like potatoes and quinoa, since the plants were protected from grazing animals and fertilized by manure. Wild quinoa was a favorite food of wild camelids, and perhaps it was the growth of undigested grain from manure patches that first suggested the possibility of farming quinoa.

Quinoa also helped feed another domesticated animal: the guinea pig. Guinea pigs offered a portable source of protein on demand, since people could carry them around in baskets. According to scholar David Wilson, guinea pigs "have a high reproductive rate, are not particularly intelligent to begin with, and can be fed discarded food scraps and grains such as quinoa."[10]

Over time, more and more species of plants were domesticated and grown. However, few animals were available for further domestication. For instance, there were no horses or oxlike animals to make farming easier by pulling carts or plows.

CORN AND ITS SISTERS

The maize plant, or corn, lay at the heart of another agricultural complex which developed in Mesoamerica. Corn began as a wild grass, familiar all over Central America, called "teosinte." In Mexican caves, ancient seed cases or cobs have been found. Archaeological dating methods have revealed that the older ones are smaller than the more recent ones, showing that people were domesticating teosinte. The process began at least seven thousand years ago, probably when people were looking for insurance against periodic droughts and the resulting food shortages. A band with enough food to eat during dry times was a band that would survive.

This corn grinding stone was made by the ancestors of the Pueblo.

Most corn was dried to allow long storage. Grinding the dried corn to make flour required special equipment. In Mesoamerica, standard grinding tools were the stone tablet, called a "metate," and the stone roller, or "mano." Ground corn was mixed with water to make tortillas or corn cakes. Natives also created hominy, which consisted of corn treated with lime to remove the hulls, then dried, and later boiled.

None of the foods made from corn contained a complete protein (unlike many seeds and nuts). However, beans or squash—also incomplete alone—provide the needed supplement to complete the corn protein. This healthful combination also worked well in the fields: The bean plants used the cornstalks for support, while squash spread on the ground in the partial shade of the cornstalks. Beans, corn, and squash became known as the essential "three sisters."

Corn growing spread, first to South America, and then into North America about the time of Christ. Domesticated animals, however, did not follow corn cultivation as llamas and guinea pigs seemed to accompany the growing of potatoes and quinoa. Two exceptions were bird species. Turkeys were domesticated in Mesoamerica and North America, and flocks of Muscovy ducks were bred for food in South America.

THE QUESTION OF STORAGE

Whatever the crop, preservation and storage were vital parts of the agricultural process. There was no point in growing a crop if it could not be saved for use when needed. Corn could be dried. In the Andes,

CORN AND HEALTH

While corn made a welcome steady food supply, it did not necessarily improve people's health. Archaeologist Wesley Cowan tells how a corn diet affected farmers called the Fort Ancient people in the Ohio River valley. This passage is from his book, First Farmers of the Middle Ohio Valley.

"Maize in some form was probably eaten day in and day out, almost 365 days of the year. The consequences of this carbohydrate-dominated diet are frightening: chronic malnutrition, excessive rates of infant mortality, and—because of crowded village conditions—increased rates of communicative disease throughout the 25 generations of Fort Ancient development. Periods of stress are reflected in interruptions in the growth of long bones and teeth. Tuberculosis and bone lesions are common in some of the Fort Ancient populations. Cavities, massive abscesses, and periodontal [gum] diseases were so common that an army of modern dentists would have been kept busy for a lifetime drilling, filling, and pulling. Overall, the Fort Ancient peoples suffered worse health than any of their predecessors. But they survived."

a kind of freeze-drying was invented for potatoes. Brian Fagan explains:

> They would leave their potatoes out in the night frost, allowing the sun to warm them by day. The family would walk over their tubers, pressing out the moisture until, after several nights, the potato became a light, white chunk. The dessicated potatoes could be stored for five or six years, easily carried in bulk, and simply reconstituted by soaking in water. *Ch'uno,* dried potatoes, are still a staple of the Andean diet.[11]

Once the crop was preserved, it had to be stored. In climates that were dry and cool enough, pits were dug under house floors or outdoors, then lined and covered to store foods and tools.

A newer form of storage was pottery —clay held together by a gritty material such as ground shell, then treated with fire until it becomes hard and waterproof. The first pottery was apparently not made by farmers, but by fish and shellfish eaters in the Amazon basin between 7500 and 4000 B.C. However, pottery certainly accompanied agriculture. A wealth of pottery shapes and decorations appeared across the Americas. Native potters held in common, however, the idea that pottery, like the harvest, was a gift from the earth. The pottery was created by the same earth which gave birth to the life-sustaining

A sample of traditional Pueblo pottery from New Mexico.

crops stored within it. Describing the North American Pueblo attitude to pottery, Tom and Richard W. Hill Sr. explain that "clay, which the Pueblo potters use to make bowls, jars, plates, vessels, and figures, is still considered to be the flesh of the living earth. . . . The Pueblos believe this gift from Mother Earth must be handled with care and sincerity,"[12] even for utilitarian pots.

AGRICULTURE AND BELIEF

As the Pueblo attitude suggests, agriculture and its accompanying changes affected the way people thought about the nature of the world. New emphasis was placed on the sun and rain, coming from the sky, and their union with the earth in making plants grow. Human fertility was linked with this cosmic fertility. The seasons, which marked the agricultural year, became more important than ever. Shamans led their bands, now in long-term camps and permanent villages, in cere-

monies celebrating the renewal. An ancient song from southwest North America expresses some of this thinking in relation to corn.

> When our earth mother is replete
>   with living waters,
> When spring comes,
> The source of our flesh,
> All the different kinds of corn,
> We shall lay to rest in the ground.
> With their earth mother's living
>   waters,
> They will be made into new beings.
> Coming out standing into the
>   daylight
> Of their sun father,
> Calling for rain,
> To all sides they will stretch out their
>   hands.[13]

In annual ceremonies, many farming people celebrated and took part in the process of renewed life and growth, offer-

This ancient vessel depicting a person weeping suggests an association between tears and rain.

A Rain Song

This Pima rain song from the arid North American west shows how agricultural needs went along with spiritual expressions. The basket drum, played along with this song, was thought to help encourage rain. This translation is from American Indian Prose and Poetry, *edited by Margot Astrov.*

Hi-iya naiho-o! The earth is rumbling
From the beating of our basket drums.
The earth is rumbling from the beating
Of our basket drums, everywhere humming.
Earth is rumbling, everywhere raining.

Hi-iya naiho-o! Pluck out the feathers
    From the wing of the eagle and turn them
Toward the east where lie the large clouds.
    Hi-iya naiho-o! Pluck out the soft down
From the breast of the eagle and turn it
    Toward the west where sail the small clouds.
Hi-iya naiho-o! Beneath the abode
    Of the rain gods it is thundering;
Large corn is there, *Hi-iya naiho-o!*
    Beneath the abode of the rain gods
It is raining; small corn is there.

ing gifts of harvested plants to the sun or the Creator. One example is the yearly Green Corn Ceremony practiced by North American tribes of the eastern woodlands. At the end of summer, the people brought fresh corn and other vegetables to the ceremonial ground to be blessed. The whole village was cleaned, the people danced, and new house fires were lit from the ceremonial fire representing the sun.

VILLAGE LIFE

The stable food supply provided by corn allowed populations to grow in agricultural villages. Rising populations also meant more competition for good farmland or scarce resources such as salt. People bumped up against others more often, so that warfare and defense became a bigger part of life. When corn growing led to large permanent villages in northeast North America, for example, the villages were fortified with stockades at territorial boundaries.

A variety of villages developed, which were more or less dependent on agriculture. Hunting and fishing remained essential to the survival of most villagers. Some people, such as those on the northern edge of the Great Plains of North America, abandoned their villages for months at a time to hunt.

Houses in agricultural villages ranged from small single-family residences, such as the white, rectangular thatched-roof houses of early Mesoamerica, to large kin-group houses, like the longhouses of northeastern North America. Other village features usually included outdoor areas used for special purposes such as games and community feasts, and a special house for ceremonies. Often the ceremonial house was also used as a council house, where leaders met.

Settled farming life led to some changes in leaders' roles. Specialist leaders developed, such as the "red chief" in southeastern North American tribes who directed the village only in times of war. Improved knowledge of plants placed still more medicinal herbs at the disposal of the shamans and healers. In Mesoamerica and in the Andes, the general leader and shaman were sometimes the same, and this figure gained power as the societies grew more complex.

Settled life made it possible for people to work for long periods at arts and crafts. In simple agricultural villages, where each family still had to produce its own food, few people could afford to work as full-time craftsmen. However, as villages grew in size and complexity, more specialists were supported by the bounty of the harvest.

AGRICULTURAL CHIEFDOMS APPEAR

With time, some groups of agricultural villages became chiefdoms. (There were also a few hunter-gatherer-based chiefdoms, in the Arctic and the Pacific Northwest, for example.) "Chiefdom" is a term used to describe a society more complex than a group of bands or villages, but less complex than a civilized state. Chiefdoms include thousands of people, who recognize one chief assisted by subchiefs. People in chiefdoms were socially ranked, and some were better off economically than others. Certainly, not all villages became part of chiefdoms. Many remained politically simple, the people in them roughly equal.

Archaeologists do not know for sure how chiefdoms began, but probably the power of leaders grew because they had the authority to distribute harvest surpluses. Traditionally, leaders were in charge of making sure all members of a band got some share of the animals hunted or the plants gathered. Agricultural surplus was handled similarly, collected from kin groups and placed in a central storehouse to be redistributed at the will of the leader.

In the same way, leaders who traditionally met with traders could control the supply of incoming goods. Archaeologists J. Pires-Ferreira and K. Flannery speak of the "enormously expanded volume of material, both raw and finished" which began to be traded when Mesoamerican villages were established. Trade goods there included "pottery, obsidian, jade, turquoise, iron pigments, shell, fish and stingray spines, shark teeth."[14] Leaders in charge of the flow of such valuable goods could use their position to reinforce the idea that they were great, even divinely inspired. At the same time, these chiefs and nobles had to show that they were of value to the people. They had to prove not only that they could distribute goods to avoid hunger and bestow prestige, but also that they would protect their people from enemies and act for their spiritual well-being.

CHIEFDOMS BASED ON CORN

Chiefdoms of many kinds existed in the Americas, but those based on corn growing were particularly large and complex. Corn growing reached the Amazon basin some time after 2500 B.C., and it transformed the narrow fertile margins of the rivers into strings of villages and gardens. One of the first European explorers described what happened when his ship approached one chiefdom of people, later called the Omagua.

> There came to receive us in the middle of the river more than 300 canoes,

A Moche jar from Peru in the shape of three maize cobs with faces.

and the one that had the fewest people carried ten, and the other, twelve Indians . . . and thus they gave the governor, Pedro de Ursua, a great gift of more than fifty canoes of fish, corn, peanuts, and yams . . . the village was very large, with more than 8,000 Indians. . . . There was in this province food for the troops, enough for more than six months, as along the riverbanks, more than four leagues upward and downward [from the village, there were] gardens of corn and sweet manioc, being a land of excellent climate.[15]

The description suggests both the wealth and size of the chiefdom and the political organization which was able to quickly launch such a flotilla of loaded boats. A description of a similar Amazon chiefdom mentions well-worn roads to the interior from the riverbanks, used by traders. The roads featured gardens carefully placed at intervals, where people bearing goods could rest and find food. The nobles and chiefs in charge of such planned prosperity enjoyed wealth and privilege. Omagua villages were each directed by a chief, and these chiefs in turn gave tribute to an overall chief, whose name meant "God." The name suggests that spiritual power reinforced political power in that chiefdom.

Other agricultural chiefdoms arose in southwest North America, among ancestors of the Pueblo people. Corn growing began there by 1200 B.C., and led in time to chiefdoms such as the one at Mesa Verde. Its organization is reflected in the beehives of thermally efficient attached houses its members built, and in the

A view of ancient attached houses at Mesa Verde National Park in Colorado shows entraces to underground kivas, or ceremonial chambers.

elaborate water engineering which helped them to farm during dry periods. At the heart of the large attached villages, called pueblos, lay kivas. These were round sunken rooms where ceremonies and dances were performed to recall the mythic history of the people, to encourage rain and harvest, and to strengthen the ties that bound people together. Not far away, at Chaco Canyon, enormous pueblo structures stood at the intersection of a set of long roads. The structures owed their existence to a trade in turquoise which drew many people from great distances. The planners of the structures gained wealth from trade, but they probably took their authority from the spiritual meaning people felt lay within the glowing, blue-green stones.

The largest city ever built in ancient North America was the center of a great chiefdom on the Mississippi River. This city, Cahokia, lay near present-day St. Louis, Missouri. Today, its chief remaining structure is a huge mound of earth, one hundred feet high and sixteen acres across. At its most prosperous, between A.D. 1050 and 1250, the city extended around the mound for over five square miles, and may have housed about thirty thousand people. The central mound was built as a platform, which held buildings that probably included a ceremonial temple and the chief's house. Other lesser platforms and burial mounds were spread throughout the city, along with plazas, houses, and outlying cornfields. Some elaborate burials and decorated objects suggest that the

APPRECIATION FOR CAHOKIA

Thomas Brackenridge was a journalist in the early American republic. His reports were read closely by Thomas Jefferson, among others. Visiting the ruins of the ancient city of Cahokia in 1811, he felt inspired. This passage is quoted by Roger Kennedy in Hidden Cities: The Discovery and Loss of Ancient North American Civilization.

The mounds at Cahokia were built between A.D. 900 and 1500.

"Nearly opposite St. Louis . . . on the banks of the Cahokia . . . [I saw two complexes containing] not less than one hundred mounds. One of the mounds falls little short of the Egyptian pyramid Mycerius. When I examined it in 1811, I was astonished that this stupendous monument of antiquity should have been unnoticed by any traveller. . . . Who will pretend to speak with certainty as to the antiquity of America—of the races of men who have flourished and disappeared—of the thousand revolutions, which, like other parts of the globe, it has undergone? The philosophers of Europe, with a narrowness and selfishness of mind, have endeavored to depreciate every thing which relates to it. They have called it the *New World*, as though its formation was [later than] the rest of the habitable globe."

residents were spiritually anchored to ancestors buried there. Plazas and temple areas may have been used by the leaders of Cahokia for the redistribution of grain in ceremonies that strengthened the hand of authority. Yet though this chiefdom was grand, it did not reach the degree of social and artistic complexity—or political strength—found in the civilizations of Mesoamerica and the Andes.

3 Civilization Begins in Mesoamerica and the Andes

After 3000 B.C., civilization began to bloom in two areas where agriculture got an early start: Mesoamerica and the Andes region. These areas were quite different from one another; but they shared qualities which allowed civilizations to arise, civilizations which were different on the surface but similar in the way they depended on already ancient ideas about the relation between groups of people and the spirit world.

CIVILIZATIONS ARISE INDEPENDENTLY

Most historians today agree that a civilization can be defined generally as a very complex society. Only six times in human history has a civilization developed without influence from another civilization. These so-called pristine civilizations arose in Mesopotamia, the Indus Valley, China, Egypt—and in Mesoamerica and the Andes region. Why here, and among these particular groups of American natives? Historians still debate the answers to these questions, but there are at least three likely reasons.

One reason for the growth of civilization in both places is the early beginning and continual improvement of agriculture. The surplus food agriculture provided allowed many people to be fed while they spent their days doing specialized work—one of the keys to civilization. In addition, large-scale agriculture required social organization, including people who planned and directed the work of large groups. That kind of organization could then be applied to other tasks, such as road or city construction.

A second reason for emerging civilization is the ease of exchange among a variety of natural regions within each area. In the Andes region, these regions include mountain grasslands and valleys, coastal strip river valleys, and the long west coast itself, rich in seafood. Mesoamerica encompasses dry northern mountains and valleys, damp southern highlands, and jungle lowlands with both Atlantic and Pacific coastlines. In each area, these varied environments, with their different resources, lay close enough for constant, lively exchange. Where resources were exchanged, ideas were traded also, contributing to a richer way of life.

Finally, both regions shared the constant threat of earthquake and drought. Cooperation and planning, necessary to civilization, may have been the behavior of residents trying to insure themselves against natural disasters.

The route from Mesoamerica to the Andes region is long and difficult, but not impossible, to travel by canoe along the coast for many days. Historians have long

THE CASE OF CARAL

Archaeologists keep finding earlier and earlier evidence of civilization in ancient Peru. The city of Caral was revealed to have existed earlier than anyone thought. This passage is from the report in Newsweek *on May 7, 2001.*

Peruvian archaeologists excavate the ruins at Caral.

"Last week archaeologists announced that [Caral] dates from 2627 B.C., the same era when Egyptian slaves were building the Great Pyramids and a full 1,500 years before scientists thought urban civilization began in the New World. 'This is the oldest human settlement of any social complexity ever found in the Americas,' says archaeologist Ruth Shady Solis of San Marcos National University in Lima, who led the excavation. Caral may therefore be 'the birthplace of New World civilization,' says archaeologist Winifred Creamer of Northern Illinois University, a member of the team. . . . Six pyramids dot the center of the city, along with two sunken plazas; eight residential neighborhoods and numerous smaller 'platform mounds' sprawl beyond . . . the largest pyramid . . . [was] probably used for religious rituals. . . . The five other pyramids may have been the equivalent of a modern city's many houses of worship—or clubs. 'The people of Caral were beginning to form social classes, and each stratum of society might have belonged to a different pyramid,' says Rocio Aramburu, who was directing excavations last week."

wondered if Mesoamerican developments influenced those in the Andes region—and vice versa. Certainly, corn and other crops from Mesoamerica were eventually grown in the Andes. Yet there is no evidence of real communication between the two areas. Peaks of civilization arose at different times in the two regions, and each culture formed its own distinct traditions.

New Building in the Andes Region

The earliest evidence of beginning civilization in the Americas lies in massive ceremonial buildings created along the coast of South America, starting about 3000 B.C. The people who built these complexes likely thought of them as elaborations on age-old ceremonial spaces used by earlier generations. Formerly, villages featured ceremonial or council houses, and areas marked out on the ground for rituals, dances, and the activities of shamans. Now, people of a large village or a set of villages assembled to create a big rectangular house of earth and stone, with many rooms inside. When the building had outlived its usefulness, or a time of renewal had come, the people filled the rooms with sacks of stones, covered the whole structure with earth, and built new rooms on top. Over time, this process resulted in a pyramid shape—a form and way of building that lasted in the Andes region for thousands of years. Around the building, the people set out round or rectangular dancing and gathering grounds.

There were probably many uses for the ceremonial buildings. Rituals were certainly conducted there to honor ancestors, to bring rain, or to renew life in the sea and on land. Offerings were brought and sometimes burned. Shamans probably intervened for the souls in the spirit world. Sometimes, the dead were buried at the centers, but at this time no grave seemed much more important than the others. This is one hint that no great authority was forcing people to work at the building projects. Instead, kin groups probably cooperated to construct a complex the whole community could use.

Later in Andean history, groups of kin called *ayllus* worked together on projects. Probably, the tradition had already existed thousands of years earlier.

The coastal people could take time to plan and build because they did not have to seek food constantly. Living at the mouths of rivers, they enjoyed a combination of river valley agriculture and a remarkable bounty of fish along the coast. The people found that the narrow arid plain between the mountains and the coast could be very fertile when irrigated by river water. And the ocean current which sweeps that coast still continues to make it one of the world's greatest fisheries. At the same time, though, every seven to sixteen years the ocean current changes temperature, a phenomenon now called El Niño, which changes the climate. The result is far fewer fish, and periods of drought or severe storm. Perhaps the desire to survive or avoid this El Niño event helped inspire the builders.

Clustered around the ceremonial centers, or sometimes a short distance from them, were traditional villages of round houses framed with wood and interlaced reeds and faced with mud and clay. While men fished or worked in the fields, women cared for children, cooked, and practiced the area's chief craft: the creation of cotton textiles. Cotton was first grown as a crop about 3500 B.C. along the coast, and it was used to fashion huge fish nets and rich fabric. The women wove familiar mythical figures and spirit-beings into the cloth. The angular shapes of the cloth figures were caused by the crisscross arrangement of threads in the fabric. It was a style that would endure, as artisans imitated woven patterns in other materials such as stone, clay, and metal.

A painted cotton textile, created in Peru between A.D. 1000 and 1470, shows a figure with an elaborate headdress flanked by felines and birds.

MOUNTAIN CENTERS AND EXCHANGE WITH THE COAST

Soon after the first coastal ceremonial centers arose, villagers in the Andes mountains began to create their own. The mountain people lived differently from the coastal people, depending for food on hunted deer, camelids, and highland crops. But the regions were connected by a pattern of exchange. Items like salt and textiles from the coast traveled to the mountains, while precious stones, obsidian, and even guinea pigs from the mountains reached the coast. This exchange is evidence of social and political contacts, and the sharing of ideas as well as goods. According to archaeologist Richard L. Burger, the building of ceremonial centers in both places "must be consid-

ered as two interrelated elements within a single developmental process."[16]

Burger also suggests that besides shaping community life, the centers showed what the participants could do: "Like the space programs of modern industrial nations, the size and quality of [the ceremonial] constructions were public displays of the productive capacity and prestige of each society, particularly in relation to that of their neighbors."[17] He adds that the organization of labor needed to build such a complex could serve a community well in other tasks, such as planting or defense. But the main reason for the building effort remained the people's desire to align their community with their ancestors, as well as other spirits and forces thought to hold sway over the world.

What Makes a Mesoamerican

Archaeologist Michael D. Coe names all the traits shared by the Mesoamerican cultures in his book The Maya.

A terra-cotta sculpture of a Mesoamerican ball player.

"All the Mesoamerican Indians shared a number of traits which were more or less peculiar to them and absent or rare elsewhere in the New World: hieroglyphic writing, books of fig-bark paper or deerskin which were folded like screens, a complex permutation calendar, knowledge of the movements of the planets (especially Venus) against the background of the stars, a game played with a rubber ball in a special court, highly specialized markets, human sacrifice by head or heart removal, an emphasis upon self-sacrifice by blood drawn from the ears, tongue, or penis, and a highly complex, pantheistic religion which included nature divinities as well as deities emblematic of royal descent. Also in all Mesoamerican religions was the idea of a multitiered Heaven and Underworld, and of a universe oriented to the four directions with specific colors and gods assigned to the cardinal points and to the center."

Religious Movements Spread

While Andean communities were building America's first monumental ceremonial centers, Mesoamerica was dotted with white-plastered farming villages, as it had been for many hundreds of years. It was not until about 1500 B.C. that a cultural tradition called Olmec spread throughout the region. A thousand years after that, in the Andes, Chavin culture spread similarly. While Olmec and Chavin were different cultural movements, both were basically spiritual. No political empire conquered all of either region's people. And while trade was essential to their spread, neither movement was simply economic. Instead, new ways of thinking and building unified people of each region around a set of beliefs.

Olmec culture began along the swampy gulf coast of Mexico, near today's Veracruz, where farmers began to import and carve stone from the northern mountains.

The swamp dwellers probably valued the permanence of stone—a material hard to come by in their land of mud and clay. The stone was sculpted into shapes and figurines to be used as part of Olmec religious practices, often buried or dropped into a spring as an offering.

Stone was also used to face and adorn Olmec ceremonial centers, which were begun after 1200 B.C. Like those of the Andeans far to the south, but different in style, the centers included pyramids, plazas, burials, and memorials.

A ritual ball game was played in a formal court by the Olmec. Rival teams reenacted mythic conflicts from the spirit world. The ball game lasted in Mesoamerica through the time of European contact —as did other Olmec practices staged at ceremonial centers. For example, Olmec statuary suggests that shamans in that society claimed to take on the jaguar form in order to act for their people in the spirit world. The human-jaguar figure may suggest that the great leaders of Olmec societies were also shamans, as they were in later Maya times.

LIFE IN THE OLMEC TRADITION

Olmec ceremonial centers such as La Venta and San Lorenzo along the Mexican gulf coast became the anchors of loosely organized realms spread across the countryside, which included farming villages, smaller elite residences, shrines, and sizable workshops where specialist crafts were practiced for ceremonial and trade use. According to historian Mari Puche, the ceremonial center was also the seat of political and religious power, where governing groups, probably family heads and shaman-leaders, organized building and crafts, directed food storage, overlooked trade arrangements, and set the schedule of rituals. The Olmec were the first to use a 260-day ritual calendar, later adopted all over Mesoamerica.

In place of the old, more equal relations among people, Olmec society distinguished sharply between common people and the ruling elite. Ordinary people continued to live as farmer-villagers, though their lives became more complicated as they traveled to observe rituals or visit

The Olmec created huge carved heads from the stone they imported from the northern mountains.

OLMEC STONE OFFERINGS AT LA VENTA

The Olmec site of La Venta features a huge Great Pyramid and other impressive architecture, but just as impressive are the offerings which were buried beneath the structures. Richard Diehl and Michael Coe describe the precious stone objects left beneath Complex A in The Olmec World: Ritual and Rulership.

"Beneath the mounds and plazas the Olmec placed a wealth of offerings and caches, including polished jade celts [decorative axe heads], at times placed in cruciform [cross] patterns; lustrous, polished concave mirrors ground from magnetite, ilmenite and other iron ores; a courtly tableau constructed of twenty-two jade and serpentine figurines and celts; and four large mask-like mosaic pavements created from hundreds of serpentine blocks placed in a yellow and orange sand matrix. The most unusual features are three Massive Offerings, large pits (one measuring seventy-seven feet on each side and thirteen feet deep) filled with hundreds of tons of serpentine blocks. . . . A nearby tomb constructed with giant basalt columns in the form of a subterranean 'log house' contained the red-pigment-impregnated remnants of two infants accompanied by a rich offering of jade figurines and jewelry."

shrines, sent family members to craft workshops, and provided crops to feed special groups. Enormous stone heads found on Olmec sites probably portray some of the elite. Puche describes their class:

> The elites wore rich vestments to distinguish themselves from the rest of the population. . . . [Sculptures] portray them with large capes, headdresses with god figures, collars and earplugs of fine stones, and other symbols of command. . . . The houses where the leaders lived . . . were located on elevated platforms over the rest of the site

or very near the ceremonial area. . . . At San Lorenzo . . . [some] had foundations and stone drains perfectly sculpted; they included enormous stone columns in their porticos.[18]

Well-traveled trade routes led north, west, and south from the original Olmec country. By the end of Olmec times, around 600 B.C., Olmec beliefs, objects, and social organization had spread all over Mesoamerica, adapted by different groups. The core of innovations made by the Olmec became the foundation of many later cultural developments.

THE EXOTIC APPEAL OF CHAVIN

About a thousand years after the earliest Olmec times, in about 460 B.C., an unusual ceremonial center was built in the Andes called Chavin de Huantar. The center was located on a major trade route, midway between the tropical eastern slope of the Andes and the coast. Before that center was built, few tropical objects or ideas appeared west of the Andean peaks. Chavin de Huantar, however, featured reliefs and sculptures of snakes, harpy eagles, caymans (relatives of the crocodile) and jaguars—all tropical forest creatures. Perhaps the reason for such borrowing was that shamans from the mountains traveled to the eastern tropics to find plants which could create visions. Evidence points to the center being an oracle—a place where people came to hear predictions of the future and other pronouncements from the spirit world. Shamans

This gargoyle from Chavin de Huantar depicts a person becoming a jaguar.

speaking for the spirits used the plants to create the visions.

Another aspect of the spiritual meaning of the Chavin center has to do with elaborate water channeling inside the main temple. Probably the channeling reflects beliefs about water which were common to people living all over the Andes region. In later Inca times, people expressed such beliefs in terms of a system which united ocean, mountains, and rivers as one. Richard Burger explains:

> According to this . . . model, the ocean is the primary source of all water, and this water is circulated by a network of underground ducts from the sea to the mountain peaks. The occasional springs appearing from the earth even in the desert or rocky highland outcrops come out of this subterranean system. Rainbows transfer the water from the high mountain peaks to the sky so that it can be made available to the fields and canals, and, eventually, to the rivers which return the water to the sea. Out of this native model grew beliefs concerning the sanctity of peaks, glacial lakes, and springs.[19]

At Chavin de Huantar, people performed rituals such as offering ocean shells to keep the water cycle going. Nothing was more important to the farmers than control of rainfall or running water.

Chavin de Huantar quickly became a destination for pilgrim-traders from the coast as well as the mountain valleys. They came bearing gifts from their homelands for the spirits and temple leaders. Their offerings enriched the center, allowing its leaders to make the center still

A Chavin gold pendant in the form of a cat, made in Peru between 600 and 400 B.C.

more elaborate and to organize workers to produce pottery and textiles using Chavin motifs to trade and to spread their beliefs. The shaman-leaders also gained control of surrounding farmland in order to feed the new ranks of temple workers and administrators. Trade and pilgrimage spread the Chavin ideas very widely, and similar centers were established. These were often temple-centered settlements surrounded by farms, about the same size as classic Greek city-states. Although the Chavin influence had waned by 200 B.C., no other set of ideas and practices was so widespread in the Andes region until the coming of the Inca empire in A.D. 1200.

MESOAMERICAN CITIES

Even though the Chavin and Olmec influences eventually faded, institutions they started continued to develop. In Mesoamerica, the Olmec-influenced center of San Jose de Magote, in the highland valley of Oaxaca, had developed a ruling elite by 500 B.C. The people of the valley then built a new town, placed at the point where three valley arms joined atop an artificially flattened mountain. It is called Monte Alban, and it was the first true city in Mesoamerica.

Why was Monte Alban high above the valley, hard to reach from below, and distant from the fields that supplied it? Its location shows the growing differences in power between village farmers and the larger city which dominated them. Monte Alban was not just a place for the elite, however; it included housing for all different sorts of people. Historian Jeremy A. Sabloff remarks that the Main Plaza, with temples, a ball court, and elaborate elite tombs, was at the forefront of the high city. Behind it, "all three hilltops on which the site was built [showed] dense occupation; terraces on the hill slopes filled with houses; fifteen residential subdivisions with their own plazas."[20]

Many of the people who lived in these city houses were neither farmers nor elite, but specialists of many kinds: minor officials, accountants, artisans, teachers, and entertainers. Their jobs depended on the requirements of the elite and on the support of the farmer below. The concentration of specialists led to a rich growth of arts and ideas. One example can be found on Monte Alban's stone slabs called stelae, engraved with some of the earliest writing in Mesoamerica. The carving is in the form of standardized pictures, called glyphs, which indicate particular people, places, and dates. One set of glyphs shows bleeding war victims—a sign of the city's might in the region.

After Monte Alban was founded, many other villages in Mesoamerica grew to become cities. The largest city in the Americas—larger even than European capitals of the time—was Teotihuacan, in the high Valley of Mexico. By A.D. 600 it hosted a population between 100,000 and 200,000. Planners gridded the city around a three-mile-long axis called "the street of the dead" (because of monuments to ancestors there). The enormous, mountain-like Pyramid of the Sun dominated the city, but all around lay six hundred other pyramids, many plazas, two thousand apartment blocks, and five hundred craft-working compounds. The whole city was painted, both in whitewash and in color —even the streets. Some of the walls were

The ruins of the ancient Zapotec city of Monte Alban in Mexico's Oaxaca Valley. Monte Alban was the first real city in Mesoamerica.

The Pyramid of the Sun in Teotihuacan, a Toltec commercial and religious center that flourished from A.D. 100 to 650.

covered with murals, showing scenes of gods and gardens. Archaeologist Rene Millon, who studied Teotihuacan for many years, writes of its glory:

> The bold self-confidence . . . in the planning and execution of this grand design points to an authority . . . that had an unchallenged prestige, with an ability to motivate masses of people and the power to mobilize and direct workers and resources on a scale that until then was without precedent in Middle America. . . . [The monumental building along] the city's vital central avenue represents a spectacular realization in stone of the values and goals of its builders, no less than the monumental use of public space in imperial Peking, ancient Rome, Paris, Versailles, Washington, or the contemporary Manhattan skyline.[21]

Several factors led to the growth of the city. One was the valuable obsidian in the region, which from early days was traded across Mesoamerica; in return, the city welcomed foreign goods, styles, and ideas. Trade was particularly easy from Teotihuacan because the city sat astride two great traditional trade routes: one that led eastward to the gulf coast, and one that led southward. Another advantage for the city was that the valley land all around proved to be wonderfully fertile under irrigation. With planning, it was possible to grow enough corn, beans, and squash to feed the huge population.

The strongest reason for Teotihuacan's magnetism, however, may have been its connection to the sacred. A cave lay beneath the great Pyramid of the Sun, a gateway to the world of the spirits, where offerings had been left for centuries. Above the cave, the Pyramid of the Sun was built along sight lines to important positions of the sun and of the star cluster called the Pleiades. Probably observations were made to tell when times were best for planting and harvest, and for other activities in the cycle of time. The sacred power built into the pyramid and other parts of the city seemed so great that the later Aztecs called Teotihuacan "the city where time began."

Warfare seems to have ended city life in Teotihuacan around A.D. 750. Enemies may have taken advantage of weakness caused by drought or overuse of the land. The population moved out into the countryside and to newer cities rising elsewhere in Mesoamerica.

AN EMPIRE IN THE ANDES REGION

Like the Mesoamericans, the people of the Andes region continued to form more complex societies after the first unifying wave of Chavin influence passed. The number and variety of post-Chavin Andean societies is great, but much can be learned by comparing examples of an empire and a city-state in the centuries before the Inca empire began.

In the first century A.D., a civilization arose along the north coastal plain which borrowed many of the old Chavin motifs, focused on military might. This society is called the Moche, after one of the river valleys which it occupied.

The Moche leaders benefited from the knowledge of elaborate irrigation farming on the coastal plain. However, coastal strip rivers are notoriously unreliable from year to year. Controlling many such rivers could reduce the risk of famine, so the Moche set out to conquer the people of one river valley after another along the coast.

Success in these empire-making wars earned the Moche great wealth, which in turn paid for civilized accomplishments. Near the modern city of Trujillo, the Moche built the Pyramid of the Sun, the largest structure created in the Americas before European contact. Moche settlements and ceremonial centers stretched mile after mile along the coastal plain. Also justly famous, Moche arts featured delicate gold metalwork and lifelike people and local animals in pottery.

Moche ceremonial centers were clearly larger and more complex than Chavin temples, and the Moche emphasized different religious practices—glorifying war and enemy suffering. Moche lords drank enemy blood from goblets and cut off prisoners' arms, legs, and heads. In the end, however, neither the fierceness nor the talents of the Moche could save their empire. Around A.D. 800, they fell victim

This Moche monkey head is made of gold and accented with turquoise and lapis.

to an astonishing series of natural disasters which included long drought, loss of fish due to El Niño, earthquakes, sandstorms, and floods.

DEVELOPMENT OF AN ANDEAN CITY

A few other empires arose in other parts of the Andes region, all smaller than that of the Moche. The Huari, for example, colonized other groups high in the Andes as they spread their novel means of irrigating terraced fields. However, cities that controlled the lands around them, in an expanded version of the Chavin city-state, were more common. The city of Tiwanaku, for example, began with a ceremonial center near the shores of Lake Titicaca in the Andes, surrounded by bog land. Planners from the growing center found a way to drain the land with a network of canals and raised fields. By A.D. 650, Tiwanaku was a city of about fifty thousand people.

The farming folk who supported the city of Tiwanaku lived in villages among their fields. Kin groups contributed a certain amount of their produce and their labor to city purposes, and received the protection and blessing of the city in return. The only people who lived in the city itself were the great lords, their many servants, and artisans who created the buildings, sculptures, pots, jewelry, metalwork, and other materials needed by the temple and the lords. The lords themselves, extremely wealthy, and with religious as well as political power, built their own palaces alongside the temple buildings and surrounded this precinct with a holy moat. As archaeologist Alan L. Kolata explains, cities like Tiwanaku were for the elite and the religious function they promoted.

> The masses rarely participated in urban culture at all, except on the occasion of public rituals. . . . Commoners flowed into these cities at prescribed moments. They can be understood as religious tourists in a kind of elite theme park that was carefully orchestrated to impart to them a sense of emotional participation in, but social segregation from, the . . . world of the elite.[22]

To the mass of farming people, the systems planned and set in place by the great lords might be limiting, but they also put food on the table. Most Andeans in the emerging civilizations, like most Mesoamericans, probably viewed themselves as participants in something greater than themselves—a community which sustained them and gave them a place in the natural and spiritual world.

4 The Inca

In 1532, Spanish captain Francisco Pizarro and his men first encountered the ruler of the Inca, the greatest empire ever created in the Andes. The emperor's arrival was as elaborate as any in the courts of Europe. Pizarro's secretary described it this way:

> First came a squadron of Indians dressed in a livery of different colours, like a chess board. They advanced, removing the straws from the ground, and sweeping the road. Next came three squadrons in different dresses, dancing and singing. Then came a number of men with armour, large metal plates, and crowns of gold and silver. Among them was Atabilba [Atahualpa, the emperor] in a litter lined with plumes of macaws' feathers, of many colours, and adorned with plates of gold and silver. Many Indians carried it on their shoulders on high. Next came two other litters and two hammocks, in which were some principal chiefs; and lastly, several squadrons of Indians with crowns of gold and silver.[23]

The majesty of the Inca ruler was not just for show. He stood at the pinnacle of a society which had created cities and temples of masterful stone architecture, systems of farms and vast storehouses which eliminated hunger, networks of roads and communications that connected every part of the empire, armies, schools, high arts, and thriving trade. Yet the empire was created less than a hundred years before the arrival of Pizarro. The Inca elite managed this feat by building on the accomplishments of earlier groups in their lands over thousands of years. The genius of the Inca was to combine and coordinate the

Atahualpa, the last Inca emperor, ruled a relatively young but powerful empire.

knowledge and traditions of the Andeans through extraordinary organization and administration.

ORIGINS OF THE INCA

The origins of the Inca people are not clearly known, but they were most likely one of many groups of people uprooted as the Huari political system fell apart. The Inca decided to try to settle in the valley of Cuzco, high in the Andes north of Lake Titicaca. Another people, the Ayarmaca, were already living in a village there, and the two rivals fought off and on over the rule of the valley for generations. At last the Inca won, and the former Ayarmaca village became the Inca city of Cuzco.

The Inca empire did not get under way until the 1400s, when the leader Viracocha conquered the area around Cuzco and created a small kingdom. In 1438, his son, Yupanqui, led the people in an epic war against the invading Chanca. As the victor and supreme ruler, he renamed himself Pachacuti, which means "He who remakes the world." Pachacuti did remake the Inca world—he organized religious practice to focus on sun worship, with himself as representative of the sun. He encouraged the idea of ancestor worship, including worship of past rulers, the Sapa Incas. He rebuilt Cuzco in the shape of a puma, with a great fortress at its head. Above all, he kept on conquering more land. His successors, Topa Inca and Huayna Capac, extended the empire to its largest size, so that it stretched from what is now Ecuador south into Argentina, Bolivia, and Chile.

Huayna Capac's sudden death led to a civil war between two of his sons.

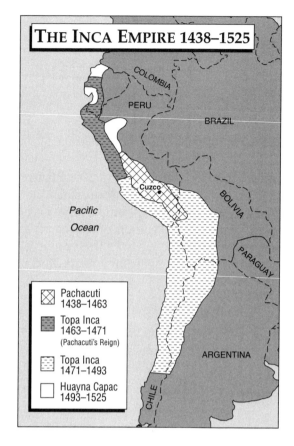

Atahualpa finally emerged as the victor. He was on his way to be crowned at Cuzco when he encountered Pizarro and his men. The empire he was supposed to inherit had been built within just four generations of Sapa Incas.

GIFT EXCHANGE: THE OIL OF EMPIRE

For thousands of years, many different tribes and ethnic groups of various sizes had developed civilization in the Andes. But none had built a huge empire like that of the Inca. The reason they were able to conquer so many other groups, and keep them in line within an empire, seems to lie largely with an ancient principle among native Americans: reciprocity, or exchange on many levels. Among the earliest bands of people, gift giving marked the mutual respect that allowed two groups to avoid conflict. In the Andes region, such reciprocity was particularly important, because people living in very different environments, from the desert coast to the mountain tops, benefited greatly when they were able to trade with one another.

Historian Maria Rostworowski points out that the Inca got a head start on goods to exchange when they defeated the Chanca. "The booty . . . must have been enormous," she says. "This large quantity of spoils was, in my opinion, the crucial factor that permitted the Inca to be 'generous,' thus oiling the gears of reciprocity."[24] Pachacuti invited neighboring lords to enjoy some of the Chanca spoils. In return, he asked them to build storehouses, then to fill the storehouses with their own

SACRIFICE OF THE CHILDREN

Archaeologist David Wilson describes how the Inca state took over ancient rites in which community would occasionally sacrifice a child to a mountain deity. This passage is from Indigenous South Americans of the Past and Present.

"To stage the *Capac Hucha,* the provinces would send each year young boys and girls, aged six to ten years old, traveling with local officials along the road system to Cuzco. Once they had all convened in the capital, the Sapa Inca and the [chief priest] would receive the children in the name of the state and the Sun religion, whereupon the boys and girls were symbolically married. Following this, the children, their provincial companions, and priests from the capital assigned to accompany them all walked back to the provinces. However, instead of following the roads on the return trip, they were required to take as absolutely a straight-line course as they possibly could, a route on which presumably the travelers encountered many hardships. Once they had returned to their home areas, the boys and girls were taken up on the highest mountaintops, wherein the [mountain deities] dwelled, and sacrificed to those deities . . . they served to ensure the fertility of the land and an abundant harvest in each provincial area where the sacrifices were carried out."

produce. Once the storehouses were full, Pachacuti could target his generosity to accomplish other feats, such as fortress building to increase Inca power.

The importance of reciprocity in keeping the empire going shows in the behavior of the emperor Huayna Capac during a war in the far north. This Sapa Inca, desperate for reinforcements, ordered one set of nobles and their troops into action without the usual feasting and gifts. The lack of reciprocity infuriated the nobles. They turned around, with their ancestral holy objects on high, and marched homeward. Huayna Capac, realizing his mistake, sent swift messengers loaded with gifts, clothes, and food. The lords were satisfied, and returned to fight alongside their emperor.

Reciprocity was rooted in the customs of Inca kin groups called *ayllus*. These village communities traditionally cooperated by working together or exchanging labor for other goods. The idea of periodic labor performed for others, called *mita*, existed before Inca times. An *ayllu* would contribute its work force if it received appropriate gifts in return.

FROM RECIPROCITY TO FORCE

Ordinary people under Inca rule might be required to do *mita* service in construction projects, mining, even weaving at home (every household had to contribute one outfit a year to the state). Most important was farming—each *ayllu* did *mita* service on lands belonging to the Inca, the temple, the local lord, and possibly others. All owners received the fruits of their own lands.

The exchange of *mita* work for security, food, or clothing was never strictly an economic one. When an individual went to perform a task, such as quarrying stone, the person was offering work for the good of the community, and this labor invited the good will of local gods or spirits as well as the great Inca Sun (the emperor).

Later in the history of the empire, as the Sapa Inca gained more power, reciprocity became less important. Instead, people were forced to work for fear of the consequences if they did not. These punishments could take various forms. Rebellious people were sometimes uprooted from their home region, separated from associates, and sent away to work among strangers. When a territory was newly conquered, some local leaders, holy objects, and even the sons of local chiefs were taken to Cuzco. One reason for this was to integrate them in the Inca system. The prisoners also could be held as potential hostages should their people misbehave back home. There were also incidents of direct force where conquered chiefs were invited to feast at Cuzco and murdered.

A HIGHLY ORGANIZED STATE

Neither reciprocity nor force could build an empire without an organized plan, and planning was certainly an Inca strong point. The entire kingdom was divided into four quarters, along lines which radiated out from Cuzco. The proper name for the empire was Tahuantinsuyu, meaning "Land of the Four Quarters." In one sense, the land was considered a body, with Cuzco as its navel. In another sense, the four quarters were administrative districts, each headed by an Inca noble, with several chiefs under him and local leaders under them. By the time Europeans arrived, the population was officially divided into groups by multiples of ten; that is, every ten families had a leader, every ten leaders had a chief, and every ten chiefs had an over-chief.

Virtual armies of administrators kept track of the work and produce of every locality. For this purpose, the Inca used elaborate color-coded knotted string devices called quipus. Huaman Poma, a native who later wrote an account for the Spanish king, detailed the duties of local lords under Inca control:

> They had to administer the provision of food, fruit-growing, garment-making, flocks and mines, whether the owner [the group to be benefited] was the community, or the poor, or the Inca and nobility, or the Sun [that is, the temples and priests]. The shepherds were under their control and they had to see that the valuable Peruvian sheep [the llamas] were counted and cared for. They had to record on the quipu the available stocks of pond-weed, dried fish, pigeon, duck, and partridge; the stocks of knives, ropes, distaffs, bobbins, and forks for digging, which all had to be wrapped and tied; and further stocks of medicinal herbs, straw, and wood.[25]

Vast amounts of goods were kept in storage houses all over the empire. These houses were relatively small, but many of them were built together in compounds. An old Andean staple, freeze-dried potatoes, filled a good number of the storehouses. Other vegetables and meats were also dried and kept in high-altitude storage where the temperature remained low. Many other supplies were also stored,

The quipu, a series of knotted strings the Inca used to keep records.

such as clothing, feathers, pottery, and arms. This storage system allowed for great flexibility within the empire. Stored goods could feed and clothe the army or work crews on building projects as needed. Supplies could easily be sent as aid from one part of the empire to another in the case of natural disaster. The goods could also support nonworkers, which included the poor, old people, priests, and nobles. Finally, the goods could reward lords or groups who had helped the Sapa Inca achieve his goals.

DUTIES OF TEENAGERS

The Inca fascination with accounting led them to try to keep track of every soul. Children were counted by age group, and each age group had its responsibilities. The Sapa Inca himself was present for ceremonies initiating children into new age groups. Hauman Poma describes the duties of the teenaged group in Letter to a King.

"In the fifth category were all those between the ages of about 12 and 18. The boys' main duty was to watch the flocks of mountain sheep [llamas]. Whilst so occupied, they learned to catch or kill a wide variety of animal life with the help of lassos, traps, and catapults.

Even before the Incas took power, boys of this age were employed in the personal service of the rulers and their divinities.

The young girls with cropped hair, who belonged to this age group, performed various useful jobs in and out-of-doors for their parents and grandparents, such as cooking and cleaning the house or helping about the farm. . . . Along with their short hair they went barefoot and wore short dresses without any elegance until they reached the age of marriage. Even then, they continued to lead the same life of poverty and service until the change from the single to the married state was ordered by the Inca or someone acting in his name. It was forbidden on pain of death for any of these girls to anticipate the order by giving themselves to a man and this was so well understood that punishment seldom had to be imposed."

Information and goods traveled along an extraordinary network of roads created under Inca supervision. One long main road went from north to south high in the mountains, while a second parallel road followed the coast. Between them ran many roads east to west, forming a kind of lattice. The roads were generally narrow, because they were meant only for foot traffic or llamas. They were paved and marked by stone walls. Spectacularly long, high rope bridges carried the roads across mountain chasms.

The Inca road system likely incorporated many old paths throughout the Andes, but the Inca organized way stations and messengers to allow efficient communication. The messengers were specially trained young men who ran in relays, often with quipus to help tell their messages. According to Poma, "a snail picked off a leaf at Tumi in the north of the Empire could be delivered to the Inca in Cuzco still alive."[26] Other messengers and llama trains carried heavy loads great distances along the road system.

MAXIMIZING PRODUCTION

To produce more and more wealth, the Inca used the best agricultural techniques developed in the Andes region, and organized workers and materials on a massive scale. In the coastal lowlands, irrigation was organized over a large territory and seabird dung was provided as fertilizer. In the mountain valleys, the Inca expanded the terracing and canal techniques of the Huari and others.

In the hard work of farming, the Inca took advantage of customs which set a festive atmosphere for group labor. "The owner of the field," said an observer, "prepares a large quantity of chicha [corn beer] for these gatherings." With drink and song, the men lined up in the field to plow, the women to break the clods of dirt. "They never miss the beat of their chant," the observer noted, "raising their [foot plows] and striking the earth with them in unison."[27] Hard work at high altitudes was also made easier when workers chewed coca leaves, which relieved pain and gave

A view of the terraces at the ancient Inca city of Machu Picchu. Terracing allowed Inca farmers to make the most of their mountainous terrain.

energy. (The Inca did not have cocaine, a modern drug derived from coca leaves.) Coca fields were sponsored by the state.

The Inca even developed an institution which encouraged production of maize beer and beautiful clothing—things traditionally made by women at home. In Cuzco, and at some provincial places, women specially chosen by the elite for their beauty and skill labored together as *aclla,* or chosen women, in a special house. There were several types of *aclla.* Some were given as wives to lords as rewards from the Sapa Inca, and some were secondary wives to the Sapa Inca himself.

The greatest surviving sign of Inca planning is the beautifully fitted stonework still standing across Peru. The Inca built forts, palaces, temples, and walls out of incredibly heavy, large stones which had to be quarried, shaped, and moved into place. The builders had no help from wheeled carts or draft animals. Their projects took huge teams of human beings, using only ropes and tools of wood and stone. The organization of labor was beyond anything ever attempted in the region before. To create the great fortress at Cuzco, for example, the Sapa Inca assembled some thirty thousand laborers.

In the Navel of the World

The planning and organization of the empire took place almost entirely in Cuzco, the capital. With a population of about 100,000, the city was the largest in South America. A visitor there would have seen many single-story houses with thatched roofs, set along narrow streets with central drainage gutters. Two rivers ran through Cuzco, made into canals with stone walls. Residents thought that

The ruins of the fortress at Cuzco. Thirty thousand workers cut, moved, and assembled the huge stone blocks to construct the fortress.

the shape of a crouching puma was formed by the rivers. Its head was on a hill above: the great fortress of Sacsahuaman. Between the imaginary paws of the puma lay a huge plaza, surrounded by palaces and ceremonial buildings. Nearby was the golden temple, the Coricancha, dedicated to the sun.

Most of the people living in Cuzco were Inca nobles, people who traced their ancestry to the first Inca to settle there. Such ancestral Inca were marked by the large earplugs they wore—the Spanish later called them "the big ears." Some other people were called "Inca by privilege," and they too were allowed to wear the earplugs and enjoy Inca status. They were from groups which had long been loyal to the Inca, or had done some great service to the state. All the top officials in the Inca government and army were "big ears."

The noble families belonged to *ayllus*, like everyone else. In Cuzco certain *ayllus* were called *panacas*. A *panaca* consisted of the relatives of a Sapa Inca who had died. The Sapa Inca Pachacuti had declared that Sapa Incas were immortal, so their lands and belongings were kept up by their relatives as though the leader were still alive. Royal mummies were brought out to the central plaza during festivals to be admired and fed. They even gave orders and made decisions, through a human agent.

The *panaca* system strongly affected the way the Inca empire grew. No new Sapa Inca could depend on inherited wealth, because anything his father had gained belonged to his *panaca*. Therefore, if he wanted his own fields and goods, each Sapa Inca had to go out and conquer new land, his wealth with which to wield power. On the other hand, the system helped control the

A gold figurine of a royal Inca secondary wife wrapped in multicolored wool.

power of the nobles over the Sapa Inca. Each one assembled his own ruling team. *Panacas* of old rulers held less and less power in Cuzco as time went on.

The lives of the nobles were luxurious. They wore finely made, elaborate garments and attended feasts, recreational hunts, and rituals. They enjoyed the hospitality of the Sapa Inca himself, who could offer such pleasures as "a courtyard full of monkeys, parrots, hawks, doves, thrushes and other birds of the Andes . . . and . . . water-gardens with fountains and fishes, and other gardens with flowers,"[28] according to Huaman Poma.

Sons of the nobility attended school for four years, where they learned language arts, religion, history, and how to count using the quipu. Girls were taught at home—especially the arts of weaving and sewing, practiced by noble and common women alike. Women were considered to have their own power and sphere, emphasized by the fact that women independently inherited wealth from their mothers, while boys inherited wealth only from their fathers.

A large number of serving people called *yana* saw to all the needs of the elite. The *yana* were born as servants, or removed from their home *ayllus* to become *yana* so that they would be loyal only to those they served.

RELIGIOUS LIFE

People of all classes shared the faith centered in the most eye-catching building in Cuzco: the Coricancha, Temple of the Sun, the spiritual center of the Inca empire. Its walls were clad in gold; they surrounded a courtyard and at least six one-room buildings. Within were many gold statues and objects, including a central garden of golden plants. In the most important room stood "an image of the sun of great size, made of gold, beautifully wrought and set with many precious stones,"[29] according to one of the Spanish invaders.

The Sapa Inca, priests, and nobles used the Coricancha to perform rituals dedicated to the sun and to plan public religious festivals. They followed a regular calendar, based largely on important agricultural events such as planting and the gathering of first fruits. The Sapa Inca and nobles themselves took major parts in rituals such as the daylong harvest sun observation noted by an early Spanish visitor.

They were all orejones [big ears], very richly dressed in cloaks and tunics woven with silver. . . . They stood in two rows, each of which was made up of over three hundred lords. . . . The [Sapa] Inca had his awning in an enclosure with a very fine seat. . . . And when the singing began, he rose to his feet with great authority and stood at the head of all, and he was the first to begin the chant; and when he began, so did all the others. . . . And so they sang from the time the sun rose until it had completely set.[30]

The sun was given great official reverence by the Inca people, but this did not mean that other deities were ignored. In fact, all the spirits and gods cherished by the people under Inca control were given respect. All across the Andean region were holy places, *huacas*, where sacrifices or offerings were made to various spirits or gods for various purposes. Many of them were tended by specific *ayllus* and visited by groups who traveled to them on pilgrimage. The tradition of shrines, holy images, and pilgrimage was an ancient one, dating at least to Chavin times. The Inca managed to organize several hundred *huacas* in the Cuzco region along imaginary lines, called *ceques*, which radiated from Cuzco. Each *ceque* intersected a number of *huacas*, like knots on a quipu string. The *ceques* were loaded with meanings. They worked as a calendar and they reflected astronomical alignments. Above all, they connected religious belief and practice to one center—Cuzco.

As the Inca elite tightened their control over the people in many ways, there was more than one sign of rebellion. A campaign to conquer people along the eastern flank of the Andes, where the tropical

What Was on the Inca Calendar

The Inca used two calendars: a daytime calendar which had 365 days, and a nighttime calendar, which used lunar months. The point of each one was to time activities and rituals. Timely actions of people in the world were considered necessary to please the deities and keep life running in the best way. These are the day and night calendar events for the summer months, as summarized by Michael A. Malpass in Daily Life in the Inca Empire.

"Daytime Calendar

June. Large potatoes were harvested and others planted.

July. Storage of potatoes and other crops; cleaning of irrigation canals.

August-September. Planting of the corn and potato crops.

Nighttime Calendar

Inti Raymi (June). Important rituals were conducted to the sun.

Chahua-huarquiz (July). Ceremonies for the irrigation systems were held.

Yapaquiz (August). Sacrifices were made to all the gods, especially those associated with the forces of nature.

Coya Raymi (September). The city of Cuzco was purified, and the sacred idols of conquered people were brought to pay homage to the king."

An Inca calendar at Machu Picchu.

forests begin, failed and had to be cancelled. The civil war just before the arrival of the Spanish reflected problems with the control and distribution of wealth. It is possible that the Inca empire would have collapsed fairly soon even without the conquest by Europeans. Perhaps the empire would have given way to a less dictatorial state or set of Andean states, still benefiting from the Inca flair for organization and planning. Or perhaps the great Inca civilization would have fallen completely, its buildings grown over, its wonders forgotten—much like the Maya, in earlier times, to the north in Mesoamerica.

Chapter

5 The Maya

The Maya developed the most sophisticated society in all Mesoamerica. Their achievements included written literature, dozens of cities, great arts, mathematics, and astronomy. Like other Mesoamericans, the Maya were strongly influenced by Olmec thinking, even after Olmec culture along the gulf coast declined about 900 B.C. As civilization grew among the Maya, they traded from their homeland in Central America with the cities of Monte Alban and Teotihuacan to the north. However, Maya city building began before either of those older cities was founded, and it continued after their fall, until about A.D. 1200.

FARMING AND TRADE IN MAYA LANDS

The ancient Maya shared the same ethnic background and spoke related languages. Their descendants, the modern Maya, still live in their ancient homeland in and around the Yucatán Peninsula. Traditional Maya lands include the southern end of Mexico, Guatemala, Belize, and parts of Costa Rica and Honduras—an area about the size of Great Britain.

Maya territory can be divided into three main regions—the southern mountainous area, bordering the Pacific, the central tropical forest area, and the drier

northern Yucatán Peninsula. Exchange among the regions was common, made easier by ties of family and language. From the southern mountains came stones including obsidian, valuable for making blades. Rich farms in the tropical forest produced cacao, used to make chocolate, cotton for textiles, and food staples such as corn, beans, squash, and chili peppers. On the northern Yucatán, villagers skimmed sea salt from drying ponds, and skilled farmers raised stingless bees for their honey—valued items for trade inside and outside Maya lands. The Yucatán

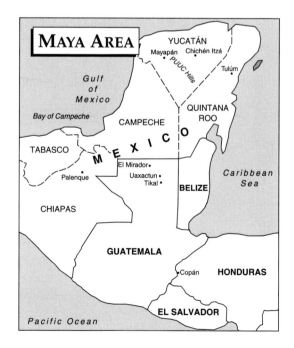

Waterways in Maya Country

Maya experts Linda Schele and David Freidel explain why waterways were so important for the growth of Maya civilization in their book A Forest of Kings.

"Spreading like the veins of a forest leaf, these waterways provided the natural avenues of travel and trade from the southern to the northern lowlands. When we think of lords visiting one another or items being traded between areas, we must remember that these people and trade goods were carried on the backs of bearers in litters or in tumplines [cloth slings that hung around the head and down the back] or in canoes paddled across the network of waterways that was the superhighway system of the ancient Maya.

These rivers were not always gentle pathways. At the height of the rainy season, especially when the great thunderstorms and the hurricanes of summer and fall sweep in from the Gulf, these slow-moving rivers can turn into raging torrents of destruction. Conversely, in the dry season they can become too shallow to navigate. Although water, overall, is abundant in the tropics, there is usually too little of it in dry times, and too much during the torrential rains of summer and fall. Because of these conditions, much of Maya social innovation was centered around two great problems: how to store excess water for the times it would be needed, and how to free wet, fertile swampland for farming."

also yielded plenty of limestone, the basis of Maya building. Limestone was not used merely as cut stone. Burnt powdered limestone mixed with water made a durable plaster, and limestone rubble mixed with clay created concretelike fill.

In spite of the ethnic ties and trade that extended across Maya country, the people were never politically united as one nation or empire. Instead, through more than a thousand years of Maya development the basis of social organization remained the village, and the city which grew from it. Cities did sometimes control land and other towns around them; but they did not unite. Maya scholars

Linda Schele and David Freidel think this local independence may have been related to the difficulty of moving large groups across the swampy central region, where many Maya cities developed. City leaders knew the swamps kept foreigners away during the wettest part of the year, and even in drier months, potential friends and invaders alike had to approach single file along treacherous paths. Schele and Freidel say that Maya city dwellers traditionally "recognized no power above their village patriarchs"[31] because the local lords were not easily unseated by outsiders.

Maya lands presented challenges to farmers as well as travelers. Slash-and-burn farming was a favored method all over the tropical forest, because it gave fresh fertility to the thin soil. As villages evolved into cities, however, the Maya also created permanent farmlands by terracing mountainsides, raising fields in swampy country, and building canals for drainage or irrigation where needed. Reservoirs stored water from the wet season for use in the dry season. These techniques helped bring prosperity, even in places that were hard to farm.

FROM VILLAGES TO CITIES

The first Maya villages to begin to resemble cities were in the southern highlands, where influences from the north were especially strong along trade routes. However, a strong wave of city building swept across the Maya central lowlands after 300 B.C. Part of the impulse to build was imported from the Olmec and other sources. But some of it was probably the local wish to become more grand, to gain more power with the gods, and to show what prosperity could do.

Evidence from the city of Cerros, located in what is today Belize, shows how one village evolved into a city. First, villagers deliberately abandoned their old homes in the town center, performing rituals of departure and then taking the houses down. They built new ones in a ring around the now-empty center. In the freed space they built a temple—a stone building set atop two stepped rectangular platforms of earth and stone. The temple pattern was already common in Mesoamerica, although the Maya added the custom of placing huge plaster decorations representing gods' faces on the fronts of the platforms. The builders soon added another temple, raised plazas, and two ballcourts.

This ceremonial precinct became the nucleus for a growing population. For the most part, Maya cities were not carefully planned, as Teotihuacan was. Instead they seemed to grow outward from the center. Many such new cities developed populations of five thousand to ten thousand, while the largest, such as Tikal, Caracol, and Calakmul, each became home to more than forty thousand people.

The immediate causes of city building among the Maya still are not certain, but one theory gives credit to a new social institution: the kingship. Villagers were used to leaders from important kin groups, but the concept of a single "ahau of the ahauob," lord of the lords, seems to have arrived at the time of city building fever. Each city's king was its ruler in politics, society, and war, as many inscriptions make clear. Equally important, however, he was also the chief religious figure. The building high at the top of the temple

Visitors climb the steps of a towering temple in the Maya city of Tikal in Guatemala.

steps was meant largely for him. There, he ingested hallucinogenic plants and pierced himself to draw blood as a sacrifice to the gods. Like other shamans, he believed himself to be transformed into the shape of a jaguar spirit who could intervene with the gods for the benefit of the city. The people, massed in the plaza below, witnessed his sacrifice, his speeches, and his ritual procession in elaborate costume through the temple and along the platform. Such drama, in such a monumental architectural setting, surely electrified a city's people and strengthened their sense of unity and purpose.

FAMILY AND SOCIAL CLASS

The king stood at the top of a highly ranked class system. Based on patterns traced among later Maya, everyone in the society belonged to one of many patrilineages, kin groups traced through the father's line. These operated as clans did for most native Americans—members

THE PURPOSES OF PYRAMIDS

Art historian Mary Ellen Miller, in this passage from Maya Art and Architecture, *points out that many pyramid temples in the Maya world were built by kings partly to memorialize their fathers. (Of course, a memorial temple or shrine could also be used to contact the spirit world.) Rich tombs were often completely sealed inside the temples. She gives the example of a large area called the "North Acropolis" at Tikal.*

"At Tikal, the North Acropolis effectively became a vast ancestral shrine over the 600 years that rulers buried their predecessors within the complex. For example, . . . Siyah Chan Kawil oversaw the interment of his father . . . he ordered a bedrock chamber be carved into the front of the North Acropolis. . . . Into the tomb went the abundance of Tikal—pots, foodstuffs, perhaps his namesake caiman . . . —alongside the dead king. Priests sacrificed nine young attendants to serve with him in the afterlife, and workmen constructed a corbel vault to seal the tomb. Then, over the next few months, a pyramid . . . rose over the tomb, to be topped by a three-chamber shrine, the rooms linked front to back, railroad-style. . . .

Freestanding pyramids seem in general to have been shrines to powerful ancestors . . . not only at Tikal but throughout the Maya realm. A king fulfilled his duty to his predecessor when he so honored him, but such constructions obviously reflected on the living as well. . . . Was it all an act of [respect for a father], or did the heir also wish to demonstrate that [his father] had outshone Hasaw Chan Kawil, whose burial in Temple 1 had [begun such building] in the eighth century? Or was the power of [the father] so great that his heir felt the need to wall him in as thoroughly as any living person could? Or, in building such a temple, did he also impress upon the neighboring cities his own absolute power, and did he force them to deliver some of the stone as tribute?"

supported and protected one another, and people had to marry outside their patrilineage. The patrilineage also held and distributed land among its members. However, while clans at other times and places in the Americas were roughly equal, the Maya ranked theirs from high to low. Maya groups also valued the ability to trace ancestry far back through noble figures on both the mother's and father's side. The term for "noble" in Mayan means "he whose descent is known on both sides."

The occupations of the nobles, men of distinguished patrilineages, are described by historian John S. Henderson:

The highest-ranking members of the most noble families filled the top positions in the rulership and priesthood. Cadet lines [not the first-born sons] and lesser aristocratic families produced lower-ranking priests and religious functionaries, scribes, long-distance merchants, architect-engineers, minor military officers, and a variety of . . . administrators. The lower echelons [ranks] of the aristocracy probably included many part-time farmers and craftsmen.[32]

Below the nobles were working commoners, including craftsmen and farmers. Probably, many craftsmen and builders were farmers who worked at other jobs during less busy seasons in the agricultural year. Many Maya artists and craftsmen produced work of such professional quality that they likely had studied and practiced, perhaps as members of families with traditions in specialty work.

Beneath the farmers socially were slaves, who were war captives or their descendants. It was possible, however, for a slave to go free if his or her patrilineage made payments to the owner.

Life in a Maya City

Day-to-day city life varied depending on a person's social class and work. Every-one lived in extended family compounds, a set of houses arranged around one or more open courtyards. For the grandest lords, the compounds were palaces with plazas. The poorest farmers lived in the same kind of small whitewashed adobe houses and central working yards that had been used in Mesoamerica for the past thousand years.

All newborn children were set in cradles with boards to flatten their heads in front and back—an effect the Maya found beautiful. People enhanced their looks by filing their teeth to points and studding them with small jewels. Upper classes wore robes or capes in addition to the standard loincloth or skirt. Elaborate head-dresses were common, especially for ceremonial occasions. Foods in Maya paintings and inscriptions include stews and tamales, packets of meat or vegetables and sauce surrounded by corn meal and steamed in corn husks. The lords probably got more kinds of food, if not more quantity, than the farmers.

At the edge of the city, the tropical forest patched with farm fields began. Peasant farmers lived along the edges of the cities, or among their fields in small villages. It was once thought that Maya cities stood isolated like islands in the damp jungle, but recent finds show many had satellite communities around them. At Caracol, for example, two rings of suburbs surrounded the city. Raised roads linked them to the center. These outlying settlements featured large market areas, buildings for administrators, independent reservoirs, and a variety of homes, with private temples for the elite.

The cities did their best to control water, which was often too plentiful or too scarce. Every city had its canals and

A pyramid and columns at Chichén Itzá, a Maya city in Mexico's Yucatán peninsula. Chichén Itzá held religious importance as a site for pilgrims.

reservoirs. In the drier northern Yucatán, deep water sources called cenotes were considered holy places from early times. The city of Chichén Itzá was built around its cenote. Even after the city lay in ruins, pilgrims went there to drop precious objects inside.

Trade in each city was regulated by the nobles but involved many private exchanges at the public market place—as it does in Mesoamerica today. Fleets of canoes moved goods long distances up and down the coasts and along the rivers.

Public events were a major part of Maya city life. The huge plazas were built to hold the people who gathered together for parades, feasts, and enactments in elaborate costumes. The events celebrated the gods, the accomplishments of the king, the creation of grand buildings, war victories, anniversaries, and calendar-related festivals.

WARFARE AND SACRIFICE

Captives were featured in ceremonies and parades because they proved the valor of Maya warriors. Warfare was celebrated in Maya society, as each city-state fought with its neighbors. Histories of kings' reigns, inscribed on stelae or walls (or, in one case, on a long flight of temple steps) emphasize their war triumphs. Historian Michael Coe describes Maya war methods:

The *holcon* or "braves" were the foot soldiers; they wore cuirasses [body armor] of quilted cotton or of tapir hide and carried thrusting spears with flint points, darts-with-atlatl, and in late Post-Classic times, the bow-and-arrow. Hostilities typically began with an unannounced guerrilla raid into the enemy camp to take captives, but more formal battle opened with a dreadful din of drums, whistles, shell trumpets, and war cries. On either side of the war leaders . . . were the two flanks of infantry, from which rained darts, arrows, and stones flung from slings. Once the enemy had penetrated into home territory however, irregular warfare was substituted, with [ambushes] and all kinds of traps. Lesser captives ended up as slaves, but the nobles and war leaders either had their hearts torn out on the sacrificial stone, or else were beheaded, a form of sacrifice favored by the classic Maya.[33]

Sacrifice was an important part of war, to show the power of the victors and to offer thanks to the gods for the victory. Sacrifice was in fact an act of daily life for the Maya, including animal sacrifice. However, the most favored form of physical sacrifice performed by the Maya was bloodletting. This practice, introduced by the Olmec, reached an extreme among the Maya. Everyone kept obsidian blades, stingray spines, or other implements to pierce the skin and draw blood. This practice, done privately and in large-scale public events, was thought to persuade gods or spirits to answer prayers. A carved scene from the city of Yaxchilan, for example, shows the king and his wife publicly letting blood. She is pulling a spine-spiked cord through her tongue. The accompanying glyphs read:

> He is letting blood . . .
> Shield Jaguar, the captor of
> Ah Ahual
> Lord of Yaxchilan
>
> She is letting blood
> name of lilies
> Lady Xoc
> Lady Batab[34]

The blood was often collected on papers, which were then burned to send a message to other worlds in smoke.

The king of the Maya city of Yaxchilan stands as his wife pierces her tongue to make a blood offering.

THE TWINS DEFEAT THE LORDS OF DEATH

The Maya myth of the heroic twins shows how clever people can influence the gods. In this part of the story, from the late Maya book the Popul Vuh, *translated here by Dennis Tedlock, the two boys are traveling in the realm of the gods, a place called Xibalba. They arrive at the court of the highest lords, One Death and Seven Death. The twins have learned the trick of seeming to kill someone, then bringing him back to life. Their plan is to kill the two lords—but not revive them. Hearing of their reputation as entertainers and musicians, the lords invite them in.*

"So they [the twins] began their songs and dances, and then all the Xibalbans arrived, and the spectators crowded the floor, and they danced everything: they danced the Weasel, they danced the Poorwill, they danced the Armadillo. Then the lord said to them:

'Sacrifice my dog, then bring him back to life again.' . . .
'Yes,' they said.
When they sacrificed the dog he then came back to life.
And the dog was really happy when he came back to life.
Back and forth he wagged his tail when he came back to life.

And the lord said to them:
'Well, you have yet to set my home on fire,'
. . . so then they set fire to the home of the lord. The house was packed with all the lords, but they were not burned. They quickly fixed it back again. . . .
'You have yet to kill a person! Make a sacrifice without death!' they were told.
'Very well,' they said.
[The boys perform the trick.]
'Sacrifice yet again, even do it to yourselves! Let's see it!'. . .
'Very well, lord,' they replied, and then they sacrificed themselves.

And this is the sacrifice of little Hunahpu by [his brother] Xbalanque. . . . His head came off, rolled far away outside. His heart, dug out, was smothered in a leaf. . . .

So now, only one of them was dancing there: Xbalanque.
'Get up!' he said, and Hunahpu came back to life. . . . One and Seven Death were as glad at heart as if they themselves were actually doing the dance.

'Do it to us! Sacrifice us!' they said. 'Sacrifice both of us!' said One and Seven Death to little Hunahpu and Xbalanque.

'Very well. You ought to come back to life. What is death to you? . . .'

And this one was the first to be sacrificed: the lord at the very top, the one whose name is One Death, the ruler of Xibalba.

And with One Death dead, the next to be taken was Seven Death. They did not come back to life. . . .

THE MAYA BELIEF SYSTEM

The practice of sacrifice was part of the elaborate Maya belief system—their view of the nature of the world around them. The Maya, like other native peoples, believed that the universe was layered, with a sky realm above, a stony middle world of earth, and a watery underworld where spirits lived. Connecting the three layers was an enormous tree—the World Tree. A creature called the Vision Serpent moved along the tree to bring one layer into being in another. This tree could be relocated to any spot where a king or priest, in a shamanistic trance, was able to re-create it and move between worlds. Linda Schele and David Freidel say the Vision Serpent "was seen rising in the clouds of incense and smoke above the temples"[35] when ritual summoned him. Essential to that ritual was the blood let by the king or priest.

The middle, earthly world was marked by the four directions, each with its own color, bird, and gods. The red-colored East, as the birthplace of the sun, was the most important. The earth also featured holy places, such as mountains or caves, which communicated with the other worlds. When people created artificial mountains (pyramids) or caves (entries to temples), they created more portals to the spirit world. This idea originated with the Olmec.

The Maya underworld was called Xibalba, and was a dwelling place of gods. It also revolved upward to become the starry sky at night. The celestial realm was thought of as a huge monster whose blood, the rain, made life possible below. Maya creation stories, later collected in a book called *Popul Vuh*, helped explain how the people thought of relations between humans and gods in Xibalba. In the most important myth, a pair of twin boys outwitted the gods and killed two of them. The story suggests that the Maya felt they could deal with the gods, given enough cleverness and special powers. Pictures of Maya kings often suggest they are related in some way to the hero twins.

MAYA WRITING

The world view that lay behind Maya civilization remains partly mysterious. But more is known about it than about beliefs of earlier Mesoamericans because the Maya revealed so much in pictures and in writing. Maya writing appears, along with pictures, on statuary and stone carvings, especially the stelae that rise from many city plazas. The Maya also created thousands of accordion-folded books made of pressed bark paper. Early sources claimed that the books included "histories, prophecies, songs, 'sciences,' and geneaologies."[36] Unfortunately, only four Maya books have survived. Most disintegrated to dust or were burned by European conquerors.

Maya writing was not decoded until the 1970s, when scholars concluded that the writing was partly hieroglyphic (a symbol representing a word) and partly phonetic (a symbol representing a sound). The written language is very flexible and full of metaphors, expressions in which one image or idea suggests others. Maya writing grew to become a complete and rich written language, comparable to the achievements of such civilizations as those of ancient Egypt or China.

Most of the written language which remains has to do with rulers and their affairs. Inscriptions on stone have allowed historians to put together a political history of the Maya central lowlands. In general, it is a story of independent warring city-states. Translating the inscriptions finally debunked the theory that the Maya once had a unified empire. However, most writing was done by specialist scribes whose duty was to tell stories from the point of view of their patron. (Art found on one vase shows scribes whose fingers were mutilated when a new ruler demanded a new version of events.) As a result, Maya history is generally one-sided, and the information from one city must be balanced against that from its neighbors.

THE CALENDAR

Many Maya books were about aspects of the elaborate calendar system, the result of centuries of development in Mesoamerica. All events, from royal actions and public ceremonies to private activities, were thought to have their proper and meaningful places in time. Sometimes an ancient date, such as the birth of an ancestor, would be deliberately changed in written records to coincide with an important later event.

Like most native Americans, the Maya thought of time as cyclical, endlessly repeating. A variety of "time loops" meshed together in the Maya system. The oldest

A stone relief containing Maya hieroglyphic script from about A.D. 775.

A Maya calendar column covered with script. According to the Maya calendar system, time was a series of cycles.

loop, the *tzolkin*, combined twenty day names with thirteen numbers to produce 260 days. The reasons for this length are uncertain. Thirteen was a favored Maya number, and twenty was the basis for the Maya counting system (probably for the ten fingers plus ten toes). The interval of 260 days is close to the average human pregnancy, and also to the length of the agricultural cycle in Mesoamerica. These facts may have had an influence.

In the Maya calendar, the *tzolkin* was meshed with another cycle, the *haab*, which ran for 360 named and numbered days, plus five year-end days. The day names and symbols of the *haab* suggest that it probably began as a farming calendar. The *haab* when meshed with the *tzolkin* created another time loop lasting fifty-two years.

As Maya civilization took hold, it occurred to leaders that a longer cycle would allow them to take a place more precisely in the march of history. They developed the "long count," which numbers the days since creation in 360-day units.

A Maya Observatory

Historian Clara Kidwell describes how the tower at Chichén Itzá called the Caracol was used for observation of celestial events. This passage is from America in 1492, *edited by Duane Champagne.*

"The Caracol resembles closely a modern astronomical observatory. It is a circular tower rising two stories above a flat-topped base. . . . It has four outer doors oriented toward the cardinal directions, and inside is a circular corridor, from which four doors open into yet another round corridor. That inner one surrounds a central core within which is a spiral staircase leading to the top of the tower. Near the top, three shafts (originally six) pierce the thick walls. These shafts serve as observing sites. They align with the vernal and autumnal equinoxes. . . . The appearance of the Pleiades in the fall and their disappearance on the date of the vernal equinox can be observed from the tower. In addition, the alignments, corresponding to the most northern and southern risings of Venus on the western horizon, allowed the prediction of . . . the first appearance of the star in the sky just before sunrise . . . on the eastern horizon."

The Caracol, the astronomical observatory at Chichén Itzá.

Creation was placed partway through the fourth century B.C. Even the long count, though, was seen by the Maya as a loop, destined eventually to repeat itself.

MATHEMATICS, ASTRONOMY, AND PREDICTION

The Maya calendars could not have operated without good mathematics. The Maya perfected a system based on the number 20, which used dots to represent one through four, a bar for five, and a stylized shell for zero. The same system must have worked well in the marketplace; but the purpose of written numbers on stones or in books were to record dates.

The surviving books all have to do with the calendar, and they also show astonishing knowledge of astronomy. One of the books, for example, includes elaborate mathematical tables showing when eclipses will occur and detailing the movements of the planet Venus. A number of Maya buildings were constructed for observing such sky events. In fact, it is possible that the Venus tables were based on observations made at the Caracol tower in Chichén Itzá. Two narrow windows in the tower provide perfect sight lines to the most northerly and southerly positions of Venus along the horizon. Clearly, Maya sages watched the sky closely, recorded what they saw, and devised mathematical models to show how patterns would repeat themselves.

The Maya followed Venus's movements because the planet was considered to be the god of war. Predicting Venus's movements allowed war planners to make the right decisions. The book with the Venus tables provides incredible detail: It tracks the planet accurately for a period of 104 years after which it repeats itself. Built into the table are glyphs which mark certain days as either fortunate or unlucky, because of the way the stars and planets are aligned. Astronomer Anthony Aveni explains how knowing the movements of Venus or other heavenly bodies, including days believed to be dangerous, may have allowed Maya people to feel they could change their fate:

> Knowing what these gods were up to was of paramount importance. Performing ritual sacrifices to them on the appropriate occasion was part of honoring a reciprocal contract. The gods help and provide for us and we pay them a debt—we offer them due compensation. Together we keep the universe in equilibrium.[37]

THE MAYA WAY FADES

Neither prediction nor sacrifice kept the Maya civilization from finally declining, as it began to do in the ninth century A.D. The reasons are not certain. Perhaps population was outstripping food production, or intercity conflict was overwhelming. A prolonged drought may have pushed people out of the cities. In any case, most were abandoned by A.D. 900. This "classic collapse" has been called one of the great cataclysms of human history. Enormous buildings, intricate stone carvings, beautiful objects—evidence of a great civilization—were left to be destroyed by the elements or covered by the jungle. A Maya poem, recorded much later in the book of *Chilam Balam*, seems to capture the feeling of this disaster.

On that day, dust possesses the earth.
On that day, a blight is on the face
    of the earth.
On that day, a cloud rises,
On that day, a strong man siezes
    the land,
On that day, things fall to ruin,
On that day, the tender leaf is
    destroyed,
On that day, the dying eyes are
    closed.[38]

However, the classic collapse did not mean the final end of the Maya. At the same time, a group of cities in the northern region emerged, notably Uxmal, Kabah, Sayil, and even farther north, Chichén Itzá. These cities shared the classic Maya features of their earlier cousins to the south. In fact, the central complex of Uxmal was perhaps the most precisely planned of all Maya cities. The northern cities lasted for another three hundred years, until about 1200, when they too collapsed. Again, the reasons are not clear. The people filtered out of the cities to other settlements, and Maya civilization faded. A lesser city called Mayapán took control of Yucatán trade for a time, but it too was gone by the time the Spanish conquerors arrived. They found a much grander living civilization to the north, in the Valley of Mexico.

Chapter

6 The Aztecs

The Aztecs were a wandering tribe before they established their own village in the Valley of Mexico between 1325 and 1345. In less than two hundred years, they created a complex civilization and the largest empire in ancient Mesoamerica. The Span-

ish adventurer who defeated them, Hernán Cortés, described their capital to his king this way:

> This great city of Tenochtitlán is built on the salt lake. . . . There are four

An illustration from an Aztec manuscript graphically depicts a human sacrifice. Hernán Cortés and other Spanish explorers who encountered the Aztecs were stunned by this practice.

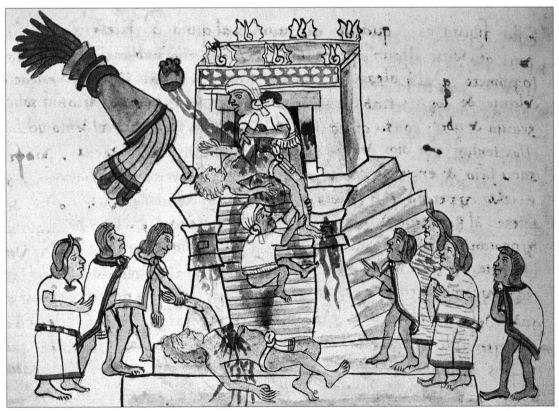

artificial causeways leading to it, and each is as wide as two cavalry lances. The city itself is as big as Seville or Cordoba. The main streets are very wide and very straight. . . .

There are, in all districts of this great city, many temples or houses for their idols. They are all very beautiful buildings. . . . Amongst these temples there is one, the principal one, whose great size and magnificence no human tongue could describe. . . . There are as many as forty towers . . . and the most important of these towers is higher than that of the cathedral of Seville.[39]

The society that produced this glorious capital sacrificed many people yearly atop the temples which Cortés had admired. A Spanish chronicler described the process:

They brought out all those who had been taken prisoner in the wars who were to be sacrificed at these festivals; accompanied closely by guards, they were made to climb those long staircases, all in rows, and totally naked, up to the place where one could see the ministers.

As they arrived in order, they were each taken by the six sacrificers, one by the foot, another by the other foot, one by the hand and another by the other, and were thrown on their back against this pointed stone, where the fifth minister threw the necklace round their throat, and the sovereign priest opened their chest with his knife, with a strange quickness, pulling out their heart with his hands and showing it, still steaming, to the sun.[40]

The fact is that the high civilization of the Aztec empire was tightly bound to the practice of human sacrifice. Both civilization and sacrifice were part of a complete world view, in which each depended on the other. This Aztec worldview grew from old Mesoamerican ideas, but took on its own unique, sometimes terrifying, character.

ORIGINS—REAL AND BORROWED

Aztec thinking reflected in many ways the history of the people. They were originally from somewhere to the north, at the outside edge of Mesoamerican cultural influence. They seem to have been hunter-gatherers who sometimes settled for a time to farm, but they were used to fighting. The men of the tribe sometimes hired themselves out to other tribes as warriors. These tough wanderers called themselves "Mexica"—the term "Aztec" was given to them later, formed from the name of their mythical island of origin.

When the Aztecs entered the Valley of Mexico in the 1100s, they found a mix of peoples already settled there in villages and cities. The Aztecs admired the ones who were more civilized than they. To gain respect, the Aztecs claimed that their ancestors inhabited great ancient cities such as Teotihuacan. Long deserted and in ruins, Teotihuacan was still a destination for pilgrims who retold the legends of its glorious past. The Aztecs saw the ancient city as the grand birthplace of their era, which they called the "Fifth Sun." (Four earlier universes, or "suns,"

Marrying and Sacrificing the Neighbors

When they were newcomers to the Valley of Mexico, the Aztecs asked the chief of a settled people, the Colhua, for his daughter to be their "sovereign" and "bride" of their deity. He agreed, but the Aztecs (meaning to honor her) actually sacrificed and skinned her. Much later, the Aztecs asked again for a Colhua sovereign, this time a grandson of the chief with some Aztec blood. Spanish chronicler Friar Duran tells of the Aztecs' appeal and the old Colhua chief's response. This passage from The History of the Indies of New Spain *is translated by Doris Heyden.*

"O great lord: we, the Aztecs . . . are enclosed in a marshy land and surrounded by a lake filled with reeds and rushes. We are alone and forsaken by all the nations. . . . Now that you have permitted us to remain here, we must have a ruler to guide us. . . . We have heard that there is a son of Opochtzin [an Aztec] here. . . . We beg of you to give him to us for our king.

The lord of Colhuacan, realizing he would lose nothing by sending his grandson to rule . . . answered thus: 'O honored Aztecs, I have heard your just petition and I find satisfaction in being able to please you. Furthermore, not only is this an honor for me but—what good does my grandson do me here? . . . But I warn you that if my grandson were a woman I would not give her to you.'"

had come into being and then perished.) When the Aztecs later built a city, it was modeled after Teotihuacan, with its orderly grid of avenues, its four districts, and its huge plazas, temples, and palaces.

Even more important to the Aztecs was the supposedly ancestral city they called Tollan (now known as Tula), the capital of the Toltec people. Like Teotihuacan, Tollan lay in ruins by Aztec times, and Toltec culture was no longer alive. The Toltecs were still featured, however, in almost mythic stories all over the Valley of Mexico. They were said to have been a race of warriors who ruled over a great domain. The Aztecs learned to speak the Toltec language, Nahuatl, which was still common in the Valley of Mexico. Reverence for Toltec ways shows in the Aztec expression "to have a Toltec heart." According to historian Richard F. Townsend, this phrase meant "to excel, to be worthy, to possess extraordinary qualities in the esteemed manner of the ancients."[41]

The actual ruins of Tula do show strong images of a warrior aristocracy, such as animal symbols of military societies and tall stone warriors atop a pyramid. Images of sacrifice include a wall where rows of rattlesnakes intertwine with skeletons. The Toltec empire was

These stone warrior columns stand on a pyramid in the Toltec capital of Tula.

probably fiction, but it seems the culture's enthusiasm for war and prisoner sacrifice, emulated by the Aztecs, was genuine.

LIVING ON THE LAKE

The Aztecs had trouble finding a home in the crowded Valley of Mexico, and they clashed with at least one group which had hosted them. They were forced onto a marshy island in one of the shallow lakes spread across the valley floor. There, according to Aztec legend, the tribal god Huitzilopochtli revealed the special sign which meant they should settle permanently on that spot—they saw an eagle perched on a cactus, eating a serpent.

The challenge of living on a marshy lake island was formidable. The Aztecs had to figure out how to grow food and how to get the many other things they

needed to sustain life. The solutions to these problems turned out to be a mixture of invention and trade.

To extend farmable land, the Aztecs turned to the earth under the lake. They built large rafts of logs, branches, and reeds, then covered them with mud from the lake bottom. These *chinampas,* or floating gardens, were anchored by stakes or trees attached to the earth. The Aztecs planted not only corn and other vegetables on them, but also long-rooting plants which would further hold the *chinampas* in place. Eventually, mud and roots filled in where water once was to make the *chinampas* actual islands. In time, the *chinampas* filled in much of the former lake surface and fed at least half the city.

The village begun at the location of the eagle and cactus grew rapidly. It was centered on the Great Temple, originally a reed house built on the location of the famous cactus. Rebuilt many times, the house became the largest city temple. The town was divided, like Teotihuacan, into four main sections. Each Aztec clan was given a place to settle. In accord with ancient tradition, each clan member was allowed a plot, and some lands were worked by all the clan members to provide for the needy, support the rulers, and keep up the temples. The Aztecs named their city Tenochtitlán, in honor of an early chief, Tenoch.

Clan heads named two overall chiefs to govern Tenochtitlán—one for external affairs, and one for internal affairs. The external affairs chief eventually became the most powerful in Aztec society, and by 1521 he was an absolute ruler.

Trade, mixed with intermarriage, supplied the city and assured more safety for the Aztecs among their neighbors. Spanish chronicler Friar Duran remarks, "They began to fill their city with people from neighboring towns and to take them in marriage. In this way they won over the people of Tetzococo and others. They treated travelers and strangers well, they invited merchants to come to the markets of Mexico with their goods."[42] Fleets of canoes ferried goods in and out of the town, but the Aztecs also built broad causeways across the shallow waters.

As the city began to grow, some Aztecs moved to another island in the lake, founding a second city: Tlateloco. Though never as large as Tenochtitlán, Tlateloco developed similarly.

THE AZTECS GAIN POWER

The Aztecs' neighbors on the lake included a powerful group called the Tepanecs. In 1371, a new strong Tepanec ruler forced many groups in the region to pay tribute. By going to war for the Tepanecs, the Aztecs paid and were eventually allowed to capture some tribute-paying *chinampa* communities for themselves. In time, Aztec warriors thought they could rebel against Tepanec power. Legend has it that they said to the Aztec civilians:

> "If we are unsuccessful in our undertaking, we will place ourselves in your hands that our bodies may sustain you, and you may thus take your vengeance and devour us in dirty and broken pots." The people then replied: "And thus we pledge ourselves, if you should succeed in your undertaking, to serve you and pay tribute, and be your laborers and build your houses, and serve you as our true lords."[43]

The battles that followed justified the warriors' daring. Two other cities, Texcoco and Tacuba, joined the Aztecs to create the Triple Alliance. These three, along with other rebellious tribute payers, overwhelmed the Tepanec capital. The Tepanec ruler was ritually sacrificed on a platform built for the purpose in his own capital. His blood was scattered in the four directions, symbolizing both the end of Tepanec power and the fertilizing of the earth for a new era.

The overthrow of the Tepanecs suddenly made a large amount of land and tribute available. The Triple Alliance divided the Tepanecs' tribute-paying lands among themselves. Although Tenochtitlán became the powerful center of the Triple Alliance empire, each city kept control of its own tribute-paying lands.

The warriors also gained personally, as they were granted land from this windfall.

TRIBUTE

Friar Diego Duran listed many of the items given in tribute to the Aztec empire by the conquered peoples. His list is quoted in Serge Gruzinski's The Aztecs: Rise and Fall of an Empire.

"And as tribute they paid a great quantity of these feathers, feathers of all types and colors: green, blue, red, yellow, violet, white. . . . Innumerable quantities of cacao; enormous quantities of cotton bales, both white and yellow.

As for blankets, there were an amazing number . . . some had great edgings worked with color and feathers; others had great emblems . . . all were worked with threads of various colors and mingled with duck and goose feathers, those tiny velvety feathers, superb and strange.

. . . there were clothes made of worked and painted cotton . . . made with great care and elegance. . . .

These nations paid tribute to the Mexicans with live birds, the most precious kind with rich plumage. . . . There were wild animals of all kinds: tribute was paid with live lions and tigers . . . they were brought in cages. Then snakes, big and small, poisonous and non-venomous, wild and tame . . . every type of shell produced by the sea was brought in tribute. . . .

Other provinces paid tribute with hollow cups . . . big plain bowls . . . or big plates for carrying food to the table and for offering water to rinse the hands . . . women's clothing, blouses and skirts . . . mats . . . seats . . . maize and beans . . . squash seeds . . . cut wood, and tree bark . . . stone, lime, wood, planks . . . moles, weasels, and big mice . . . fruits . . . roses . . . armour made of cotton . . . bows, arrows . . . honeycombs. . . .

And those provinces lacking in provisions, clothing and all the above, paid tribute with young women, girls and boys, whom the lords shared [as slaves] among themselves."

Two great war leaders received ten units of land each, commanders of lesser rank got two, and clan leaders were granted just one unit for the upkeep of their temples. This was a major change from the way land had been distributed when Tenochtitlán was founded. The power of the clan leaders to control land was greatly reduced, while the warrior class gained in wealth, power, and social rank. Every conquest after that served to strengthen the hand of the warriors in Aztec society.

CREATING AN EMPIRE

Itzcoatl, the victorious Aztec ruler, was not slow to begin increasing the size of the new empire. Often, armies from the three allies worked together, or two would cooperate. Sometimes an army from one city would conquer alone with the permission of the others. By the time the Spanish arrived, the empire included most of central Mexico, from the Atlantic to the Pacific—although there were unconquered areas within it.

Leaders of the empire allowed rulers of conquered areas to remain in power in return for certain tribute. After battle, Aztec negotiators set the tribute when they learned what the people had on hand, be it blankets, feathers, gold jewelry, wild animals, firewood—nearly anything could serve as tribute. People who could not give anything else gave up children to be used as slaves.

Tribute was paid to a variety of authorities. In joint military ventures, each Alliance city received goods from a portion of the lands. Each city's part was then divided for use by temples, army, government, leaders, and aristocrats. Tribute record books show how much work it must have been to collect all the tribute and send it to the appropriate places and people. To the warriors themselves, tribute was a great reward; but the greatest reward of war was the return to Tenochtitlán with a chain of captives to be sacrificed.

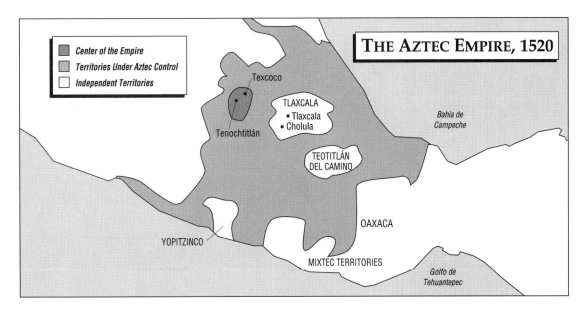

THE MEANING OF HUMAN SACRIFICE

Human sacrifice had many meanings for the Aztecs. On a practical level, it frightened potential enemies into submission. Leaders of territories the Aztecs wanted to control were invited to Tenochtitlán regularly to witness the death of Aztec enemies. The sacrifice of captives also had a mythic past among the Aztecs. Captives were killed atop the pyramid of the Great Temple of Tenochtitlán partly in memory and imitation of the Aztec god Huitzilopochtli. Myth said that when he was born on top of a mountain, fully grown and armed, he instantly slaughtered his evil half-sister and four hundred other half-siblings.

The Aztecs also shared the widespread Mesoamerican attitude toward sacrifice, which saw it as noble for both victorious warriors and their prisoners. A chief aim of battle was not to kill the enemy immediately, but to capture him for ritual killing. It was proper for a defeated fighter to say to his opponent, "You are my beloved father," suggesting that the victor had a legitimate right to sacrifice him to the gods. The victor would reply, "You are my beloved son." Both were cooperating in the process.

Mesoamericans in general thought that human blood or human life offered to the gods helped keep the world in balance. Archaeologist Brian Fagan says that sacrifices in the ancient tradition "were

An Aztec priest holds up a sacrificed prisoner's heart. The Aztecs believed human sacrifice was necessary to maintain the balance of the world.

An Aztec Hymn

At ceremonies, hymns were chanted to honor the gods. This one is directed to Tezcatlipoca, "Giver of Life," described here as both a poet and a scribe who can create—and blot out what he created. This song is quoted in Michael E. Smith's The Aztecs.

With flowers you write,
Oh, Giver of Life!
With songs you give color,
with songs you shade
those who must live on the earth.

Later you will destroy
eagles and tigers [jaguars];
we live only in your painting
here, on the earth.

With black ink you will blot out
all that was friendship,
brotherhood, nobility.

You give shading
to those who must live on the earth.

Later you will destroy
eagles and tigers [jaguars];
we live only in your painting
here, on the earth.

not so much an expression of fear, or even an attempt to placate angry deities. They were the fulfillment of an obligation to return food and energy from society to the earth, the sky, and the waters."[44]

Under the Aztec regime, however, the amount of sacrifice grew and grew. It was fueled largely by the warrior cult which had the society in its grip. The need for sacrifices demanded continual wars of conquest. Fifty years before the arrival of the Europeans, Tenochtitlán witnessed an unprecedented orgy of sacrifice. For four days in a row, captured victims were led steadily up temple steps to be killed. The blood pooled in the plazas. Enormous skull racks reminded everyone of how many had been killed in the past. Those days of sacrifice fed into the old Aztec prediction that the end of their era of the Fifth Sun was approaching, and that the only way to keep time from stopping was to continue to sacrifice more and more people.

The Gods and Their Landscape

Sacrifice was one of many rituals the Aztecs performed to stay in accord with

The Aztec calendar system dictated when agricultural events and religious festivals would occur. Pictured here is an Aztec calendar manuscript.

their world. Most (though not all) sacrifice was devoted to the sun. The old Aztec god, Huitzilopochtli, encouraged sacrifice to the sun, just as he encouraged conquest. The other two chief Aztec gods were Tlaloc, an ancient Mesoamerican rain god, and the feathered serpent, Quetzalcoatl, who represented wind and storms brought by the wind. The Aztecs honored other deities with rituals, festivals, parades, and singing.

The natural landscape of Tenochtitlán was the backdrop for such actions. The city of Tenochtitlán was sacred to the Aztecs, not only because it was the place where their deity told them to live, but also because the island surrounded by water represented the earth. Mount Tlaloc, near Tenochtitlán, seemed to catch rain clouds that brought life-giving water to crops. A temple was established on the

mountain, to which the Aztec king made regular pilgrimages. Other locations also housed shrines such as "Tree-thorn Place," an extinct volcano.

The created landscape of the city, especially its holy center, formed another, carefully created environment. Like earlier Mesoamerican temples, Aztec shrines were pyramid-shaped, suggesting mountains. The chief artificial mountain of the city, the Great Temple, had two houses at its top—one a shrine to Huitzilopochtli, and the other to Tlaloc. Below the pyramids lay large plazas like plains used for gatherings and processions.

The Aztecs moved around these landscapes largely in accord with a calendar-based round of festivals and observances. They used the same Mesoamerican calendar as the Maya: a 260-day calendar, consisting of eighteen months of twenty days each, and a 360-day count with five extra days at its end. Festivals were held at the end of every twenty-day period, and numerous activities were connected with other days. As had the Maya, the Aztecs particularly tied the 360-day count to agriculture. Friar Duran remarked, "These characters [of the calendar] also taught the Indian nations the days on which they were to sow, reap, till the land, cultivate corn, weed, harvest, store, shell the ears of corn, sow beans and flax seed."[45]

At certain times, the calendar called for spectacular use of the sacred landscape. For example, the end of a complete fifty-two-year cycle called for special renewal. All fires were put out. Then, as certain stars rose, a fire was started on the chest of a sacrificial victim at Tree-thorn Place. Meanwhile, a giant tree trunk, first raised at the Great Temple, was brought by boat out to a certain spot in the lake. A procession carrying torches brought the light down from the mountain and then by boat across the lake, illuminating the tree trunk which had been set in the lake bottom and raised high to represent the Tree of Life. The torchbearers then continued to the city to relight the temple and all the household fires. This ceremony renewed both time and the meaningful landscape in which the people lived.

Daily Living

Despite constant warfare, human sacrifices, and the apparent approach of the end of the Fifth Sun era, ordinary Aztec people lived pleasant daily lives. Most people lived in simple adobe houses. Lords and their servants lived in many-room palaces. In the countryside, farmers toiled in the fields or tended the *chinampas* from canoes. In Tenochtitlán and other Aztec cities, however, the wealth of empire made it possible for many people to work as craftsmen or to live the life of the warrior-lord.

In town, the Aztec day was punctuated by men blowing conch horns at intervals to indicate the time. The main meal of the day was eaten in midafternoon. A nap followed. The food of the working people was simple, but the lords ate very well. Tamales of many kinds were popular, and everyone's favorite drink was chocolate prepared in a variety of ways, often with chilis or spices.

Children growing up in the cities went to school. Each clan kept a school connected with its temple where children memorized many things and learned how to give speeches. There were no books at school, because Aztec hieroglyphics were meant to be read only by experts. Chosen children of aristocrats attended special schools to learn to be leaders and religious specialists.

Singing and dancing were important subjects in both kinds of schools. The Spanish friar Mendieta commented:

One of the principal things that was in all the land were the songs and dances, both to solemnize the feasts . . . and for private enjoyment and solace. Each lord had in his house a chapel with composer-singers of dances and songs, and these were thought to be ingenious in knowing how to compose the songs in their manner of meter and couplets that they had. Ordinarily they sang and danced in the principal festivities that

Aztecs dance at a celebration of the new year. Singing and dancing were popular in the Aztec empire, for both festivals and private recreation.

were every twenty days, and also on other . . . occasions. The most imporant dances were in the plazas; on other occasions in the houses of the lords, as all the lords had large patios.[46]

As they grew up, boys and girls came to live separate lives. Men and women did not normally eat meals together, for instance, even if they were married. For boys, the arts of war were glorified. The Mesoamerican ballgame was played for sport, but boys also went to watch ritual ballgames at the great stone city courts, where the losers were often sacrificed. Young warriors sometimes took part in "flower wars," so named because richly attired warriors fell on the battlefield like flowers. These wars were prearranged ritual fights against other cities for captives. The warriors fought one pair at a time. It was a chance for a warrior to gain captives for sacrifice, and make a name for himself— though he himself risked capture and death. It is a measure of the strength of the war culture of the Aztecs that the flower wars always attracted volunteers. Yet in the end just a few hundred Europeans overwhelmed this culture of proud warriors. The Europeans represented a force from a completely different world—one the Aztecs could not understand or handle.

Chapter

7 Contact and Conquest

When Christopher Columbus landed on the Caribbean island of Hispaniola in 1492, he led a flood of Europeans who poured into the Americas in the following centuries. To the natives, it was like an invasion from outer space. They had no idea who these people were, and they tried in vain to fit them into their belief systems. And the Europeans had no bet-

ter understanding of the natives. They viewed them as children, animals, and inferiors—a few saw them as angels. Almost immediately, the first contacts turned into conflict. The meeting of peoples became a conquest, in which the long heritage of the natives was destroyed, buried, or ignored—though it was never entirely snuffed out.

Natives of Hispaniola offer Christopher Columbus presents after his historic landing on the island.

DISEASES KILL MILLIONS OF NATIVES

Many natives felt the first terrible impact of contact before they even laid eyes on Europeans. Disease microbes spread from tribe to tribe far inland while the newly arrived Europeans were still at the coasts. The native people had never encountered European viruses before, and so they had none of the natural immunity Europeans enjoyed. Smallpox in particular spread rapidly after 1492, first in Mexico and then in South and North Amer- ica. No records survive of most of the deaths; but they probably resembled those among the Aztecs:

> It was [the month of] Tepeilhuitl when it began, and it spread over the people as great destruction. Some of it quite covered [with pustules] on all parts—their faces, their heads, their breasts, etc. There was a great havoc. Very many died of it. They could not walk; they only lay in their resting places and beds. They could not move; they could not stir; they could not change position, nor lie on one side; nor face down, nor on their backs. And if they stirred, much did they cry out. Great was its destruc- tion. Covered, mantled with pustules, very many people died of them.[47]

Eighty percent or more of all native Americans probably died of diseases like this within a few decades of the first European arrivals.

The "Great Dying," as historian Roger Kennedy names it, caused not only physical damage, but also great cultural damage. Those most likely to die in the epidemics were the weakest individuals, including the older people. Elders were the most experienced leaders, and the ones who knew best the oral histories, tales, songs, and formulas which formed the cultural heart of the people. A Maya lament from an epidemic of the 1520s cries: "Your grandfathers died, and with them died the son of the king and his brothers and kinsmen. So it was that we became orphans, O my sons!"[48] Even though populations eventually rose again, those elders were not there to pass on their knowledge to the next genera- tion. Leaders were not there to guide the people through the difficult times ahead. Europeans did not mean to cause this harm. But it was the beginning of a process which the Europeans continued —the process of separating natives from their own culture.

THE PATTERN OF SPANISH AND PORTUGUESE CONQUEST

Just two years after Columbus landed on Hispaniola, the pope as head of the Cath- olic Church arranged an agreement be- tween the great powers of Spain and Portugal. The Treaty of Tordesillas di- vided the "new world" oceans and lands, still mostly unexplored by Europeans, be- tween the two countries. Portugal was to have the area of what is now Brazil, plus the trade route to India. Spain was to have the rest of the Americas. In fact, Spain stayed mostly in Central and South Amer- ica, because great riches in gold and silver were found there. As part of the treaty, the pope urged Spain and Portugal to convert all the natives they encountered to Catholic Christianity.

The kings of Spain and Portugal commissioned expeditions to explore the new lands and find out what profitable resources they might have. The chief motive for coming to the Americas was economic, although the religious conversion of the people was also important. Captains of these expeditions, later called conquistadors, sought out wealth among the natives and forced them to submit to European authority.

The conquistadors carried with them the tremendous power of European technology. The natives found it hard to defend themselves against horses, metal armor, metal swords, and spears—weapons they themselves did not have. The Europeans also used firearms, cannons, and arquebuses (a kind of musket). An Aztec informant later told the Spanish friar Sahagun about the firing of a cannon in Tenochtitlán:

> Then the Spaniards fired one of their cannons, and this caused great confusion in the city. The people scattered in every direction; they fled without rhyme or reason; they ran off as if they were being pursued. It was as if they had eaten the mushrooms that confuse the mind, or had seen some dreadful apparition. They were all overcome by terror, as if their hearts had fainted. And when night fell, the panic spread through the city and their fears would not let them sleep.[49]

As this passage suggests, the technology had both a practical and a psychological effect, frightening people into submission. It allowed relatively few armed Europeans

Christopher Columbus could be viewed as the first conquistador.

to overwhelm many thousands of natives, both in these early conflicts and over the next several hundred years.

Columbus himself could be seen as the first conquistador. He forced natives to work on estates in the Caribbean islands, which he took for himself and his entourage. These islands became a headquarters for expeditions to the mainland and for Spanish trade ships.

THE AZTECS AND MAYA FALL

The conquest of the mainland began in earnest in 1519, with conquistador Hernán Cortés's voyage to Central America. Cortés was attracted by tales of Aztec wealth; but he plotted his approach carefully since he had also heard of the Aztecs' awesome armies. As he neared the coast, he found that local people despised the

Hernán Cortés rallies his soldiers. Cortés and his army were able to take Tenochtitlán due in part to the damage smallpox wreaked on the Aztecs.

Aztecs for forcing those they conquered to pay tribute and give up people for sacrifice. Cortés made allies among these victims of Aztec power as he approached the capital in the central mountains.

When Cortés arrived at Tenochtitlán, the Aztec emperor, Montezuma II, greeted him as an honored visitor. Montezuma thought that Cortés in fact was the god Quetzalcoatl. Old predictions said the god would come to the city one day from the East. Cortés did not deny this; he accepted the emperor's hospitality. Then, Cortés was called back suddenly to the coast to deal with another group of Spanish arrivals. When he returned to Tenoch-

titlán, he found the city in revolt because his lieutenant, Pedro de Alvarado, had killed some Aztecs. In a chaotic night, called "la noche triste" (the sad night), the Spanish force fought its way out of the city. Cortés rallied an army of seventy thousand from among the groups who hated Aztec rule. With Cortés's five hundred Spanish soldiers, they lay siege to Tenochtitlán. The city fell within three months, mostly because the population was ravaged by smallpox.

With the authority of the Spanish king, Cortés and his officers converted the Aztec empire into the center of a Spanish colony. Because the people of the empire were used to obeying central authority and to making payments, they fell in line with Spanish law and taxes. Tenochtitlán became Mexico City, capital of the Viceroyalty of New Spain.

From the conquered capital, Cortés and then Alvarado went south to take the lands of the Maya. There, the going was not easy. Although the Maya civilization was past its prime, settlements did remain, full of fierce fighters and surrounded by swamps. Cortés's officer Pedro de Alvarado had better luck in the Maya highlands. He terrified the people, burning or hanging leaders who would not produce gold and silver for him to take away.

Spanish authority was established, as the remaining elite of the Maya lost their old pattern of life and thought. The knowledge contained in Maya books was destroyed in Spanish fires. Bishop Landa of the Yucatán wrote: "We found a large number of books in these characters, and, as they contained nothing in which there were not to be seen superstition and lies of the devil, we burned them all, which they regretted to an amazing degree, and which caused them much affliction."[50] The books were perhaps the last real tie to classic Maya civilization. After the 1500s, the Maya lost knowledge of their own written language.

THE CONQUEST OF SOUTH AMERICA

Another conquistador, Francisco Pizarro, led the conquest of the Inca empire. In 1532, he left the coast with only 180 men and thirty horses to find the Inca capital. After a long, difficult journey inland, the Spanish force finally encountered the Inca leader, Atahualpa, at the mountain city of Cajamarca. Boldly, Pizarro took Atahualpa

---

CORTÉS IN THE MAYA SWAMP

Looking to conquer the Maya, Cortés had to navigate the swamps that helped protect Maya city-states. He described part of his advance through the central lowlands in 1524 in this passage quoted by John Henderson in The World of the Ancient Maya.

"After having marched for three days through a dense forest along a very narrow track, we reached a great lagoon more than five hundred paces wide. . . . When all the men and horses had finally crossed this lagoon, we came upon a great marsh which lasted for two crossbow shots, the most frightful thing the men had ever seen, where the unsaddled horses sank in up to their girths until nothing else could be seen; and in struggling to get out they only sank in deeper, so that we lost hope of bringing a single horse out safely."

prisoner while his men frightened off the Inca forces with gunfire. Then Pizarro held Atahualpa hostage until his followers collected a whole roomful of gold. The gold, however, only whetted the greed of the Spanish. They strangled Atahualpa instead of releasing him and went on to sack other Inca cities.

Frightened by the Spaniards, and horrified by the murder of their god and king, the Inca people offered little resistance. Pizarro and his men completely subdued the capital, Cuzco, in 1533, stripping the Temple of the Sun of its gold sheathing and decorations. Items of gold or silver, regardless of their exquisite form or spiritual meaning, were melted down into bars to take back to Spain. A half-brother of Atahualpa was set up as a puppet king by the Spanish for a few years, but when he

Pizarro looks on as Atahualpa is baptized at the stake. Pizarro had the Inca emperor strangled after the baptism.

The Spanish Warning

As the Spanish conquest proceeded, an official warning was devised for officials to read to native peoples they encountered. It is quoted in 500 Nations, *edited by Alvin M. Josephy Jr.*

"We ask and require of you . . . to acknowledge the Church as the ruler and superior of the whole world, and the high priest called the Pope and in his name the King [of Spain] as lords of . . . this terra firma. . . . [If you submit], we . . . shall receive you in all love and charity, and shall leave you, your wives and children, and your lands, free without servitude. But if you do not [submit] . . . we shall powerfully enter into your country, and shall make war against you. . . . We shall take you, and your wives, and your children, and shall make slaves of them . . . and we shall take away your goods and shall do you all the harm and damage we can."

tried to rebel, he was killed. From a capital established by the Spanish at Lima on the coast, the Viceroyalty of Peru ruled over the old Inca empire.

On the far side of South America, the Portuguese were also quick to subdue the natives. In the 1530s, the king of Portugal gave feudal rights to twelve people, each of whom had absolute power over a huge area in Brazil called a "capitania." These Portuguese owners tried to force the natives in their regions to work on their sugar plantations, but many of them sickened and died while others fled to the interior. The Portuguese began importing slaves from Africa to work the farms, a practice that continued even after the capitanias were abolished in 1640. Some escaped slaves created their own free settle- ments in the interior or joined Indian ones. Any native settlement of any size or wealth, however, became a target of Portuguese looting and control.

Farms, Mines, and Churches

Most Spanish and Portuguese conquerors and colonists disregarded or despised native cultures and beliefs. Their European culture had taught them that their own religion, race, and economic system were superior to any in the world. Moreover, some native practices such as Aztec human sacrifice horrified the Europeans. Most genuinely felt the American Indians would be better off under a European system. Yet the European system was often as destructive of human life as that of the Aztecs, and on a larger scale.

The conquest of Mesoamerica and South America was followed by colonists' attempts to wrest more wealth from the land. Farming was one method. Large estates could ship valuable cargo to Europe for sale. In Central America and elsewhere, the Europeans took over whole villages of native people in the *encomienda* system. Its basis was tribute—familiar to many natives. The native farmers were forced to work the fields and send most of their produce to the owner. Europeans also brought in herds of animals new to the natives: sheep and cattle. In Mexico and elsewhere, grazing animals were given precedence over native farmers, and former farmland was destroyed.

Mining was another straightforward way to make land produce wealth. Once American Indian posessions had been melted down to make gold and silver ingots, the Europeans looked for the sources of precious metals in the earth. Native Americans were enslaved or made to work for very little in mines in Central America, the Andes, and Brazil. Practices used there did not always comply with European laws, but the mine operators were far from Europe and made their own rules. Inca chronicler Huaman Poma complained in vain about Andean mine conditions to the Spanish king in 1613:

At the mercury mines of Huancavelica the Indian workers are punished and ill-treated to such an extent that they die like flies and our whole race is threatened with extermination. Even the chiefs are tortured by being suspended by their feet. Conditions in the silver mines of Potosi and Chocllococha, or at the gold-mine of Carabaya, are little better. The managers and supervisors, who are either Spaniards or half-castes, have virtually absolute power. There is no reason for them to fear justice, since they are never brought before the courts. Beatings are incessant. The victims are mounted for this purpose on a llama's back, tied naked to a round pillar or put in stocks. Their hair is cut off and they are deprived of food and water during detention.[51]

The Catholic Church played a strong role from the beginning in the colonization of the southern Americas. Conversion of the natives was often used as an excuse to rob and control the populace. However, church authorities sincerely wanted to make the people Christians. They did this partly by taking over shrines once dedicated to Indian deities. It was standard practice in Central America, for example, to flatten the main pyramid in a city or village and replace it with a church. For their part, many natives were willing to incorporate the Christian God, his son Jesus, and the Virgin Mary into the collection of deities they already recognized. Among the most understanding Europeans were the priests who worked to learn native languages and tried to improve the lives of their flocks.

A DIFFERENT PATTERN IN NORTH AMERICA

In North America, Europeans and natives interacted differently. The French and English sought wealth like their neighbors to the south. But they hoped to gain it from trade with the American Indians—or from use of unpopulated land.

The fur trade proved a strong early profit maker for Europeans in the north. Jacques Cartier first claimed the Canadian region for France in a set of voyages between 1534 and 1542. The French soon realized that the most valuable material around their territory, the St. Lawrence River and the Great Lakes, was the pelts of local animals which could be sold in Europe to make coats and hats. By the 1600s, the demand for beaver in particular soared as broad-brimmed fur hats became fashionable. French merchants traded guns, blankets, and other items with local Iroquois for furs. The merchants established a network of suppliers and forts that extended far to the west from their Canadian headquarters. Soon the French merchants were competing for the trade with British-backed companies.

European fur traders did not generally try to take the American Indians' land, but the fur trade altered native ways of life all across North America. Individuals and tribes vied for the furs, sometimes ignoring other aspects of tribal life and violating ancient territorial boundaries. War among tribes broke out in the mid-1600s when the Iroquois tried to extend their trading territory. "They come like foxes through the woods," said one observer of the Iroquois. "They attack like lions. They take flight like birds, disappearing before they have really appeared."[52] Thousands died in these "beaver wars."

CLASHES OVER LAND

British claims in North America had begun in 1584, when Queen Elizabeth granted Sir Walter Raleigh the right to claim

Sir Walter Raleigh claimed much of North America for England in 1584.

any lands in North America not inhabited by Christians. Raleigh reported with some surprise that some of the non-Christians were "in their behaviour as mannerly, and civill, as any of Europe."[53] From the time of the first permanent British settlement at Jamestown in 1607, there were instances of good will between settlers and North American natives. The shared Thanksgiving feast at Plymouth in 1621 may be the most famous example. But conflict was much more common. Wars and Indian raids followed the frontier borders as settlers moved westward—and as France and Britain rallied Indian allies. In the 1600s alone, these conflicts included two Powhatan Wars in Virginia, the Pequot War

Chief Joseph (ca. 1840–1904), leader of the Nez Percé.

and King Philip's War in New England, and King William's War in Canada.

Conflict between settlers and American Indians resulted partly because of different attitudes toward the land. In most of North America, tribes were part farmers, part hunter-gatherers. They occupied large territories within which they moved seasonally. Europeans, seeing Indians come and go, got the idea that they did not have permanent homes. To the Europeans, only settlement, individual landholding, and farming of land suggested a right of ownership. These attitudes were summarized in 1758 by the author of a book called *Law of Nations.*

> It is asked whether a nation may lawfully take possession of some part of a vast country, in which there are none but erratic nations whose scanty population is incapable of occupying the whole. . . . [The Indians'] unsettled habitation in those immense regions cannot be accounted a true and legal possession; and the people of Europe, too closely pent up at home, finding land of which the savages stood in no particular need, and of which they made no actual and constant use, were lawfully entitled to take possession of it, and settle it with colonies.[54]

This attitude, mixed with the desire for land and its riches, led to continual takeover of Indian territory, and constant violation of agreements and treaties. The Indian point of view, calling for the right to move about, was summarized later by Chief Joseph of the Nez Percé:

> All men were made by the same Great Spirit Chief. They are all brothers. The

NATIVE UNITY

Tecumseh was a Shawnee chief who tried to unite tribes to keep settlers from coming west of the Appalachian Mountains. He is quoted in The Way: An Anthology of American Indian Literature.

Shawnee leader Tecumseh (ca. 1768–1813) opposed the spread of settlers to native American land west of the Appalachian Mountains.

"Will we let ourselves be destroyed in our turn without a struggle, give up our homes, our country bequeathed to us by the Great Spirit, the graves of our dead, and everything that is dear and sacred to us?

I know you will cry with me, 'Never! Never!' . . .

The way, and the only way, to check and to stop this evil, is for all the Redmen to unite in claiming a common and equal right in the land, as it was at first and as it should be yet; for it was never divided, but belongs to all for the use of each. . . . The White people have no right to take the land from the Indians, because they had it first, it is theirs. . . . It belongs to the first who sits down on his blanket or skins, which he has thrown upon the ground, and till he leaves it, no other has a right."

earth is the mother of all people, and all people should have equal rights upon it. You might as well expect the rivers to run backward as that any man who was born a free man should be contented when penned up and denied liberty to go where he pleases. If you tie a horse to a stake, do you expect he will grow fat? If you pen an Indian up on a small spot of earth, and compel him to stay there, he will not be contented, nor will he grow and prosper.[55]

The battles of the 1600s in North America were only a preview of armed and cultural clashes which continued for many generations.

Change on Both Sides

Contact and conquest altered the course of history not just for natives of the Americas, but for Europeans as well. In 1512, Pope Julius II decreed that Indians were people descended, like Europeans, from Adam and Eve. His decision was typical of a time when the Europeans were trying to adjust to the existence of previously unknown lands and people. The encounter with the New World provided endless subjects for arts, writing, philosophy, and scientific investigation. Moreover, the wealth returned from the mines, farms, and furs of the Americas, much of it gained through native labor, helped finance European courts, aristocrats, merchants, and the Catholic Church through the late Renaissance and beyond. However, the greatest gift of the American natives to Europe may have been their expertise with valuable crops. Historian William H. McNeill points out the special advantages of corn (maize) and potatoes in European fields:

> Maize and potatoes had a fundamental advantage over the different sorts of grain that Old World farmers already knew. With suitable growing conditions, they produced more calories per acre—sometimes very many more. Take the north European plain for example. Throughout that region . . . rye was the only grain that could be depended on to ripen in the short and often rainy summers. . . . But potatoes thrived in such a climate and could ordinarily produce about four times the number of calories per acre that rye did. This meant that across the vast plain of northern Europe four times as many people could live on the produce of the soil when they learned to eat potatoes instead of bread.[56]

The higher population fed by American-origin crops eventually helped make possible the rise of industrialism in Europe, and, in McNeill's words, "Europe's rise to dominion between the eighteenth and twentieth centuries."[57]

Positive changes also occurred among the natives as the result of European contact. Learning about the rest of the world, although in limited ways, opened new perspectives for natives. On a practical level, European animals were often a boon. For example, the horse, introduced by the Spanish, transformed buffalo hunting culture on the North American plains well before the pioneers arrived. The pig went wild all over North and South America, and became a very rewarding source of meat for people who kept pigs or hunted them. European technology brought new conveniences such as the wheel which eased the toil of farming and many other jobs. To some natives, the Europeans brought welcome new ideals such as Christian mercy. However, for the most part, native cultures suffered and stumbled under the impact of contact and conquest. The course of the future for all native Americans had radically changed.

Notes

Chapter 1: Hunters and Gatherers

1. Tom D. Dillehay, "A Late Ice-Age Settlement in Southern Chile," *Scientific American,* October 1984, p. 111.
2. Thomas F. Lynch, "Differentiation of Hunter-Gatherer Cultures," in Frank Saloman and Stuart B. Schwartz, eds., *The Cambridge History of the Native Peoples of the Americas, Vol. 1, North America.* Cambridge, England: Cambridge University Press, 1999, p. 149.
3. David J. Wilson, *Indigenous South Americans of the Past and Present.* Boulder, CO: Westview Press, 1999, p. 140.
4. Wilson, *Indigenous South Americans of the Past and Present,* p. 117.
5. Kenneth M. Morrison, "Religion," in Duane Champagne, ed., *Native America: Portrait of the Peoples.* Detroit: Visible Ink Press, 1994, p. 456.
6. Quoted in Denise Lardner Carmody and John Tully Carmody, *Native American Religions: An Introduction.* New York: Paulist Press, 1993, p. 42.
7. Morrison, "Religion," *Native America: Portrait of the Peoples,* pp. 441–42.
8. Quoted in Alvin M. Josephy Jr., ed., *America in 1492: The World of the Indian Peoples Before the Arrival of Columbus.* New York: Alfred A. Knopf, 1992, p. 366.

Chapter 2: The Practice and Impact of Agriculture

9. Brian M. Fagan, *Kingdoms of Gold, Kingdoms of Jade: The Americas Before Columbus.* London: Thames and Hudson, 1991, p. 88.
10. Wilson, *Indigenous South Americans of the Past and Present,* p. 84.
11. Fagan, *Kingdoms of Gold,* p. 90.
12. Tom Hill and Richard W. Hill Sr., eds., *Creation's Journey: Native American Identity and Belief.* Washington, DC: Smithsonian/National Museum of American Indians, 1994, p. 175.
13. Quoted in A.L. Soens, ed., *I, The Song: Classical Poetry of Native North America.* Salt Lake City: University of Utah Press, 1999, p. 233.
14. Kent V. Flannery, ed., *The Early Mesoamerican Village.* New York: Academic Press, 1976, p. 286.
15. Quoted in Anna Roosevelt, ed., *Amazonian Indians from Prehistory to the Present.* Tucson: University of Arizona Press, 1994, p. 82.

Chapter 3: Civilization Begins in Mesoamerica and the Andes

16. Richard L. Burger, *Chavin and the Origins of Andean Civilization.* London: Thames and Hudson, 1995, p. 42.
17. Burger, *Chavin and the Origins of Andean Civilization,* p. 38.
18. Mari Puche, "Life in Olmec Times," in Michael D. Coe et al., *The Olmec World: Ritual and Rulership.* Princeton, NJ: Princeton University Press/Henry N. Abrams, 1996, p. 39.
19. Burger, *Chavin and the Origins of Andean Civilization,* pp. 111–12.
20. Jeremy A. Sabloff, *The Cities of Ancient Mexico: Reconstructing a Lost World.* London: Thames and Hudson, 1997, p. 56.
21. Quoted in Sabloff, *The Cities of Ancient Mexico,* p. 62.
22. Alan L. Kolata, ed., *Tiwanaku and Its Hinterland.* Washington, DC: Smithsonian Institution Press, 1996, p. 280.

Chapter 4: The Inca

23. Quoted in Carmen Bernand, *The Incas: People of the Sun,* trans. Paul G. Bahn. New York: Henry N. Abrams, 1994, pp. 130–31.
24. Maria Rostworowski de Diez Canseco, *History of the Inca Realm,* trans. Harry B. Iceland. Cambridge, England: Cambridge University Press, 1999, p. 40.

25. Huaman Poma, *Letter to a King: A Peruvian Chief's Account of Life Under the Incas and Under Spanish Rule,* trans. and ed. Christopher Dilke. New York: E. P. Dutton, 1978, p. 99.

26. Poma, *Letter to a King,* p. 100.

27. Bernabe Cobo, *Inca Religion and Customs,* trans. and ed. Roland Hamilton. Austin: University of Texas Press, 1990, pp. 212–14.

28. Poma, *Letter to a King,* p. 95.

29. Quoted in Fagan, *Kingdoms of Gold, Kingdoms of Jade,* p. 45

30. Quoted in Brian S. Bauer and David S. P. Dearborn, *Astronomy and Empire in the Ancient Andes: The Cultural Origins of Inca Sky Watching.* Austin: University of Texas Press, 1995, pp. 22–23.

Chapter 5: The Maya

31. Linda Schele and David Freidel, *A Forest of Kings: The Untold Story of the Ancient Maya.* New York: William Morrow, 1990, p. 57.

32. John S. Henderson, *The World of the Ancient Maya.* Ithaca, NY: Cornell University Press, 1997, p. 144.

33. Michael D. Coe, *The Maya.* New York: Thames and Hudson, 1987, p. 160.

34. Quoted in Fagan, *Kingdoms of Gold, Kingdoms of Jade,* p.118.

35. Schele and Freidel, *A Forest of Kings,* p. 69.

36. Coe, *The Maya,* p. 161.

37. Anthony Aveni, *Stairways to the Stars: Skywatching in Three Great Ancient Cultures.* New York: John Wiley and Sons, 1997, p. 121.

38. Quoted in Coe, *The Maya,* p. 154.

Chapter 6: The Aztecs

39. Hernán Cortés, "Letters from Mexico, 1519–1526," in Serge Gruzinski, *The Aztecs: Rise and Fall of an Empire,* trans. Paul G. Bahn. New York: Henry N. Abrams, 1992, p. 166.

40. Jose de Acosta, "Natural and Moral History of the Indies" (1590), in Gruzinski, *The Aztecs,* p. 158.

41. Richard F. Townsend, *The Aztecs.* London: Thames and Hudson, 2000, p. 46.

42. Quoted in Townsend, *The Aztecs,* p. 66.

43. Quoted in Townsend, *The Aztecs,* p. 73.

44. Fagan, *Kingdoms of Gold, Kingdoms of Jade,* p. 28.

45. Quoted in Townsend, *The Aztecs,* p. 133.

46. Quoted in Townsend, *The Aztecs,* p. 172.

Chapter 7: Contact and Conquest

47. Quoted in Alfred W. Crosby Jr., *The Columbian Exchange: Biological and Cultural Consequences of 1492.* Westport, CT: Greenwood Press, 1972, p. 56.

48. Quoted in Crosby, *The Columbian Exchange,* p. 58.

49. Miguel Leon-Portilla, ed., *The Broken Spears: The Aztec Account of the Conquest of Mexico,* trans. Lysander Kemp. Boston: Beacon Press, 1992, p. 66.

50. Quoted in Henderson, *The World of the Ancient Maya,* p. 13.

51. Poma, *Letter to a King,* p. 135.

52. Quoted in Alvin M. Josephy Jr., *500 Nations: An Illustrated History of North American Indians.* New York: Alfred A. Knopf, 1994, p. 233.

53. Quoted in Josephy, *500 Nations,* p. 187.

54. Emerich von Vattel, *Law of Nations; or Principles of the Law of Nature, Applied to the Conduct and Affairs of Nations and Sovereigns* (1758), trans. Joseph Chitty. Washington, DC: Carnegie Institution of Washington, 1916, p. 85

55. Chief Joseph, *An American Indian's View of Indian Affairs* (1879). Kirkwood, MO: The Printery, 1973, p. 43.

56. William H. McNeill, "American Food Crops in the Old World," in Herman J. Viola and Carolyn Margolis, eds., *Seeds of Change: Five Hundred Years Since Columbus,* Washington, DC: Smithsonian Institution Press, 1991, p. 45.

57. McNeill, "American Food Crops in the Old World," in *Seeds of Change* p. 52.

For Further Reading

Books

Andrea Due, Renzo Rossi, and Martina Veutro, *Civilizations of the Americas.* New York: Macmillan Library Reference USA, 1996. A large and beautiful atlas with many maps of different times and places in the Americas, along with drawings, text, and some statistics.

Joy Hakim, *A History of US: Book One, The First Americans.* New York: Oxford University Press, 1993. A reliable and delightful overview of natives of the United States at the time of European contact, with the story of their first meetings with Europeans.

Mathilde Helly and Remi Courgeon, *Montezuma and the Aztecs.* Trans. Hilary Davies. New York: Henry Holt, 1996. A lighthearted book about the Aztecs: each double-page spread is on one topic, such as "The Garland Wars: They Only Sound Pretty," with creative graphic illustrations.

Anna Lewington, *What Do We Know About the Amazonian Indians?* New York: Peter Bedrick Books/Simon and Schuster, 1993. The text of this large-format book is simple, but it features excellent pictures of such timeless details of Amazonian life as manioc bread.

Carolyn Meyer and Charles Gallenkamp, *The Mystery of the Ancient Maya.* Rev. ed, New York: Margaret K. McElderry Books/Simon and Schuster, 1995. An excellent and thorough view of the Maya, told as a set of mysteries and their unraveling.

A. LaVonne Brown Ruoff, *Literatures of the American Indian.* New York: Chelsea House, 1991. This is a book about the native North American oral tradition and other record keeping, such as paintings and songs. Includes many poems and other literature, and explains the ways they are part of ongoing Indian life.

Helen Roney Sattler, *The Earliest Americans.* New York: Clarion Books, 1993. Richly illustrated with sepia drawings, this large-format book is especially good on the first migration to North America and the lives of the Paleo-Indians.

Ray Spangenburg and Diane K. Moser, *American Historic Places: The American Indian Experience.* New York: Facts On File, 1997. This guide book tells about ancient Indian sites which can be visited within the United States.

Tim Wood, *The Incas.* New York: Viking, 1996. Large-format double-spread illustrations vividly show aspects of Inca life.

Videos

Michael Barnes, "Secrets of Lost Empires: The Inca." Videocassette produced for *Nova* television series. South Burlington, VT: WGBH Video, 1997. This video shows in detail how the Inca managed to move heavy stone and create mortarless walls which withstood earthquakes and the ravages of time.

William A. Brown, *Fall of the Aztec and Maya Empires.* Chicago: Questar Video, 1999. Covers the Spanish conquest and follows the journeys of an American explorer in 1839. This video describes many of the cities of ancient Mesoamerica, using computer graphics to show the buildings as they once were.

Edward S. Curtis, *In the Land of the War Canoes*. New York: Milestone Film and Video, 1972. A classic film by a great photographer of Northwest Coast Indians, made in 1916, when many were still living traditionally. It has been restored and an authentic Kwakiutl chant recording added.

The Mystery of Chaco Canyon. Olney, PA: Bullfrog Films, 1999. Robert Redford narrates this video about the meaning of the ancient buildings in Chaco Canyon, New Mexico. The work includes contemporary Pueblo interpretations and computer reconstructions.

Time-Life's Lost Civilizations. Vol. 2: *Maya*, Vol. 9: *Inca*. Alexandria, VA: Time-Life Video and Television, 1995. Two volumes from the ten-volume series on ancient civilizations help bring the Maya and Inca to life.

Works Consulted

Books

Walter Alva and Christopher B. Donnan, *Royal Tombs of Sipan*. Los Angeles: Fowler Museum of Cultural History, UCLA, 1993. The catalogue and accompanying essays for a museum display. This book includes gorgeous photos of objects made by the Moche of the Andean region and explains their sacrifice ceremony.

Margot Astrov, ed., *American Indian Prose and Poetry*. New York: John Day, 1972 (reproduction of 1942 edition). A classic collection of mainly North American Indian literature.

Anthony Aveni, *Stairways to the Stars: Skywatching in Three Great Ancient Cultures*. New York: John Wiley and Sons, 1997. A professional astronomer's analysis of knowledge of the stars among the people of ancient Britain, the Maya, and the Inca.

Brian S. Bauer and David S. P. Dearborn, *Astronomy and Empire in the Ancient Andes: The Cultural Origins of Inca Sky Watching*. Austin: University of Texas Press, 1995. This learned book explains in technical detail the lines of sight to astronomical phenomena used by the Inca, and the place that knowledge of astronomy had in their culture.

Elizabeth P. Benson, *The Mochica: A Culture of Peru*. New York: Praeger, 1972. A scholarly source on the Moche people with excellent pictures, especially of pottery, real people, and daily life, but little about more recent discoveries of tombs revealing sacrifice details.

Elizabeth P. Benson and Beatriz de la Fuente, eds., *Olmec Art of Ancient Mexico*. Washington, DC: National Gallery of Art, 1996. This large-format book catalogues a major Olmec art exhibit and includes interpretive essays.

Carmen Bernand, *The Incas: People of the Sun*. Trans. Paul G. Bahn. New York: Henry N. Abrams, 1994. An account of the Incas that emphasizes their encounters with Pizarro and includes excellent pictures and original documents.

Richard L. Burger, *Chavin and the Origins of Andean Civilization*. London: Thames and Hudson, 1995. The best scholarly account of Chavin culture and its aftereffects, with large photographs.

Denise Lardner Carmody and John Tully Carmody, *Native American Religions: An Introduction*. New York: Paulist Press, 1993. The authors explain the thinking and feeling behind North American Indian religions, sympathetic both to natives and to contemporary people trying to understand them.

Duane Champagne, ed., *Native America: Portrait of the Peoples*. Detroit: Visible Ink Press, 1994. This book includes individual essays on each of many tribes of North America followed by chapters on aspects of native cultural life.

Bernabe Cobo, *Inca Religion and Customs*. Trans. and ed. Roland Hamilton. Austin: University of Texas Press, 1990. An excellent primary source on Inca life.

Michael D. Coe, *The Maya*. New York: Thames and Hudson, 1987. A classic work on the

Maya, thorough but readable; it is regularly updated in fresh editions.

Michael D. Coe et al., *The Olmec World: Ritual and Rulership.* Princeton, NJ: Princeton University Press/Henry N. Abrams, 1996. This art book catalogs an exhibit of Olmec art. The large photographs are accompanied by essays on Olmec life and ways by leading scholars.

C. Wesley Cowan, *First Farmers of the Middle Ohio Valley.* Cincinnati, OH: The Cincinnati Museum of Natural History, 1987. This booklet explains how one group of agricultural villagers lived in the Ohio Valley.

Alfred W. Crosby Jr., *The Columbian Exchange: Biological and Cultural Consequences of 1492.* Westport, CT: Greenwood Press, 1972. A readable book full of facts about every aspect of the biological exchange between the Americas and Europe, from smallpox to corn, in the context of worldwide biological diversity.

Fray Diego Duran, *The History of the Indies of New Spain.* Trans. Doris Heyden. Norman and London: University of Oklahoma Press, 1994. Father Duran lived and worked in Mexico in the 1500s, and wrote books about the Aztecs based on native sources. His accounts and illustrations are of great value because they were written so close to the time of the events.

Brian M. Fagan, *Kingdoms of Gold, Kingdoms of Jade: The Americas Before Columbus.* London: Thames and Hudson, 1991. This book leaps around periods but emphasizes unifying themes and tells many thrilling stories about the ancient cultures.

Kent V. Flannery, ed., *The Early Mesoamerican Village.* New York: Academic Press, 1976. A collection of archaeologists' research into agricultural villages in ancient Mexico, much of it technical.

Serge Gruzinski, *The Aztecs: Rise and Fall of an Empire.* Trans. Paul G. Bahn. New York: Henry N. Abrams, 1992. Beautiful and authentic pictures, a large section of primary documents, and exciting stories about the Aztecs.

Evan Hadingham, *Lines to the Mountain Gods: Nazca and the Mysteries of Peru.* Norman: University of Oklahoma Press, 1987. This book introduces the Nazca culture, which drew enormous lines and pictures on the southern coastal part of the Andes region before Inca times. The author suggests that the lines reflect many common aspects of Andean regional culture.

Ross Hassig, *War and Society in Ancient Mesoamerica.* Berkeley and Los Angeles: University of California Press, 1992. A scholarly work that details the purposes and methods of war in Mesoamerica, especially among the Maya, the Aztecs, and in Teotihuacan.

John S. Henderson, *The World of the Ancient Maya.* Ithaca, NY: Cornell University Press, 1997. This is a complete scholarly work on the Maya.

Tom Hill and Richard W. Hill Sr., eds., *Creation's Journey: Native American Identity and Belief.* Washington, DC: Smithsonian/National Museum of American Indians, 1994. This beautiful book includes art and words from a wide variety of Native Americans, mostly from North America, and mostly since European arrival.

Chief Joseph, *An American Indian's View of Indian Affairs* (1879). Kirkwood, MO: The Printery, 1973. In this speech, first published as an article in *North American Re-*

view, Chief Joseph of the Nez Percé spoke feelingly of the plight of his own tribe, and of Native Americans in general, under U.S. rule.

Alvin M. Josephy Jr., ed., *America in 1492: The World of the Indian Peoples Before the Arrival of Columbus.* New York: Alfred A. Knopf, 1992. This thorough history includes good pictures of many different ways of life in ancient America on the eve of Columbus' arrival.

———, *500 Nations: An Illustrated History of North American Indians.* New York: Alfred A. Knopf, 1994. This classic history reads easily and is full of wonderful illustrations.

James H. Kellar, *The Atlatl in North America.* Indianapolis: Indiana Historical Society, research paper, June 3, 1955. A short paper on the nature and historic use of the atlatl, or spearthrower.

Roger Kennedy, *Hidden Cities: The Discovery and Loss of Ancient North American Civilization.* New York: Free Press, 1994. This intriguing book traces mound building in North America from its beginnings around 3000 B.C. and documents the "discovery" of these ancient constructions by European-Americans.

Alan L. Kolata, ed., *Tiwanaku and Its Hinterland.* Washington, DC: Smithsonian Institution Press, 1996. A fascinating scholarly book about the culture of an early pre-Inca city-state.

Miguel Leon-Portilla, ed., *The Broken Spears: The Aztec Account of the Conquest of Mexico.* Trans. Lysander Kemp. Boston: Beacon Press, 1992. Leon-Portilla assembled testimony from a variety of historic sources to put this account together; the stories are wonderfully immediate and very moving.

Michael A. Malpass, *Daily Life in the Inca Empire.* Westport, CT: Greenwood Press, 1996. This book describes daily life in Inca lands in a straightforward way.

Mary Ellen Miller, *Maya Art and Architecture.* London: Thames and Hudson, 1999. This analytical work includes beautiful pictures of Maya buildings and objects, many in color.

W.S. Penn, ed., *The Telling of the World: Native American Stories and Art.* New York: Stewart, Tabori, and Chang, 1994. This large book includes beautifully presented art and stories from many centuries of North American native life.

Huaman Poma, *Letter to a King: A Peruvian Chief's Account of Life Under the Incas and Under Spanish Rule.* Trans. and ed. Christopher Dilke. New York: E.P. Dutton, 1978. (Ms. written between 1567 and 1615.) This immediate and easy-to-read work includes the author's delightful drawings of people engaged in various tasks in the Inca empire.

Heather Pringle, *In Search of Ancient North America.* New York: John Wiley and Sons, 1996. A journalist visits ancient sites where discoveries about early Americans have been made.

Anna Roosevelt, ed., *Amazonian Indians from Prehistory to the Present.* Tucson: University of Arizona Press, 1994. Scholarly essays fill this book about the people of the Amazon region.

Maria Rostworowski de Diez Canseco, *History of the Inca Realm.* Trans. Harry B. Iceland. Cambridge, England: Cambridge University Press, 1999. This book presents one archaeologist's view of how the Inca empire got started.

Jeremy A. Sabloff, *The Cities of Ancient Mexico: Reconstructing a Lost World*. London: Thames and Hudson, 1997. Short essays describe eight Mesoamerican cities, each accompanied by an imagined scenario showing what life there might have been like.

Frank Salomon and Stuart B. Schwartz, eds., *The Cambridge History of the Native Peoples of the Americas*. Vol. I, *South America, Part 1*. Cambridge, England: Cambridge University Press, 1999. One of the most up-to-date and reliable reference works about all ancient South American peoples, with explanatory essays.

Linda Schele and David Freidel, *A Forest of Kings: The Untold Story of the Ancient Maya*. New York: William Morrow, 1990. This book made a tremendous splash in Maya studies. It is a readable account of relatively recent knowledge about the Maya, including their writing system and kingship.

Michael E. Smith, *The Aztecs*. Malden, MA: Blackwell, 1996. A standard history of the Aztecs, with quotations from primary sources.

A.L. Soens, ed., *I, The Song: Classical Poetry of Native North America*. Salt Lake City: University of Utah Press, 1999. Poetic texts, most originally sung or chanted, passed down from generation to generation in North American tribes.

Karen Spalding, *Huarochiri*. Stanford, CA: Stanford University Press, 1984. A scholarly work on the Huari people, who built an empire predating the Inca.

Dennis Tedlock, trans., *Popul Vuh: The Mayan Book of the Dawn of Life*. New York: Touchstone/Simon and Schuster. Rev. ed., 1996. Religious stories collected by Europeans well after the peak of Maya civilization, but probably of ancient origin.

Richard F. Townsend, *The Aztecs*. London: Thames and Hudson, 2000. A thorough and reliable account of the Aztec culture, including archaeological evidence.

Bruce G. Trigger and Wilcomb E. Washburn, eds., *The Cambridge History of the Native Peoples of the Americas*. Vol. I, North *America, Part 1*. Cambridge, England: Cambridge University Press, 1996. An excellent scholarly reference work with essays on periods of development in North America before 1492.

Emerich de Vattel, *The Law of Nations, Or, The Principles of Natural Law*, Vol. 3. Trans. Charles G. Fenwick from the edition of 1758. Washington, DC: Carnegie Institution of Washington, 1916. A historic treatise demonstrating European thought about land rights in the 1700s and earlier.

Herman J. Viola and Carolyn Margolis, eds., *Seeds of Change: Five Hundred Years Since Columbus*. Washington, DC: Smithsonian Institution Press, 1991. Beautifully illustrated essays about the biological exchanges (of plants, animals, and diseases) between the Americas and the rest of the world that occured after 1492, including effects on such distant places as Africa and China.

David J. Wilson, *Indigenous South Americans of the Past and Present*. Boulder, CO: Westview Press, 1999. This book draws many fascinating connections between peoples of ancient South America and their modern descendants, in the interest of constructing a theory to help explain why cultures change.

Shirley Hill Witt and Stan Steiner, eds., *The Way: An Anthology of American Indian Literature*. New York: Alfred A. Knopf, 1972. This anthology includes many famous political statements by Native American leaders, both historic and more recent.

Periodicals

Tom D. Dillehay, "A Late Ice-Age Settlement in Southern Chile," *Scientific American*, October 1984. Archaeologist Dillehay presents evidence of plant use among Paleo-Indians at Monte Verde.

"New World Pyramids," *Newsweek*, May 7, 2001. This article describes the discovery of Caral in the Andes region, one of the earliest known cities there.

Kenneth B. Tankersley, ed., "Special Report: The Puzzle of the First Americans," *Scientific American Discovering Archaeology*, February, 2000. The most recent evidence for the time and manner of arrival of the first people in the Americas (at the time of publication) is explained in this series of articles, which also detail the attitudes of contemporary Indians.

John Noble Wilford, "In Maya Ruins, Scholars See Evidence of Urban Sprawl," *New York Times*, December 19, 2000. This article describes the discovery of ancient suburbs to Maya cities.

John Noble Wilford, "Study of Ancient Indian Site Puts Early American Life in New Light," *New York Times*, September 19, 1997. This article describes the uncovering of the earliest known mound complex in North America.

Index

Julius II (pope), 98

Kabah, 74
Kellar, James
  on the atlatl, 20
Kennedy, Roger, 35
  on damage of smallpox
    to natives, 88
Kidwell, Clara
  on observatory at Caracol, 72
Kingdoms of Gold, Kingdoms of Jade
  (Fagan), 17
King Philip's War (New
  England), 96
King William's War (Canada), 96

Lady Batab, 67
Lady Xoc, 67
Lake Titicaca, 48, 50
La Venta, Mexico, 41
  riches of, 42
Law of Nations
  on Indian and European
    attitude toward land, 96
Letter to a King (Poma), 54
Lima, Peru, 93
Lynch, Thomas, 16

Machu Picchu, 27, 59
Malpass, Michael A.
  on Inca calendar, 59
Maya
  agriculture and, 60, 62
  artisans and professionals and,
    65
  astronomy and, 72–73
  belief system of, 68
  climate and, 61
  fading away of, 73–74
  life in city of, 62, 65–66
  natural resources of, 60
  social structure and, 63–65
  trade and, 60–61
  written literature and, 10, 60,
    69–70
Maya, The (Coe), 40
Maya Art and Architecture (Miller),
  64
Maya Highlands, 91
Maya of Cerros, 9
Mayapán (city), 74
McNeill, William H.
  on advantages of corn and
    potatoes, 98
Mesa Verde, 33–34
Mesoamerican civilization
  cities of, 44–47

corn and, 28
disease and, 10
domestic animals of, 28
glyphs and, 45
natural threats to, 36
origins of, 36–37
traits of, 40
Mesopotamia, 36
Mexico City, 91
Miller, Mary Ellen
  on purpose of pyramids, 64
Million, Rene, 46
Mississippi River, 34
Moche (Andean society), 47–48
Monte Alban (Mesoamerica)
  class structure, 44
  cultural development, 45
  Maya trade with, 60
Monte Verde
  plant materials in diet at, 14
Montezuma II, 90
Mount Tlaloc, 84

native Americans
  Christianity and, 89, 94
  destruction of history of, 10
  European culture and, 93–94
  European technology, effect
    on, 89
  migration, 8, 12, 31
  rise of industrialism and, 98
  tools of, 8, 13
  types of societal groups of,
    9–10
*Native America: Portrait of the
  Peoples* (Champagne), 18
natural resources
  of Andes, 38
  fertile land as, 60
  forests, 14–15
  of Mesoamerica, 32
  mining of, 94
  obsidian, 6
  stone and, 41
  of Yucatán Peninsula, 61
Navajo, 22–23
New Spain, 91
Nez Percé, 96
North America, 94–96
North American Indians
  fur trade and, 95
  guessing games and, 18
  Salmon settlers of, 17
  Thanksgiving and, 96
  unity of, 97
Northern Illinois University, 37
Nukak, 16–17

Oaxaca Valley, 44
Okanagan people, 9
Old Crow River, 15
Olmec, 40–44
  architecture and, 62
  natural resources of, 42
  religious nature of, 40
  social structure of, 41
*Olmec World: Ritual and Rulership,
  The* (Diehl and Coe), 52
Omagua people, 33
Ona, 20–21

Pacific Northwest, 23
Paleo-Indians
  archaeology and, 15
  bands of, 16
  role of humans in nature and,
    23
  settlements and, 24
  tools of, 13–14
  tribes, 16
Penn, W.S., 9, 23
Pequot War, 96
Peru, 20
Pima Indians, 31
Pizarro, Francisco, 49, 91
plants
  domestication of, 25–26
  of "Eastern Agricultural
    Complex," 25
  end of ice age and, 13–15
  psychotropic, 21, 63
  tropical forest of Maya empire,
    60
Plymouth, Massachusetts, 96
political organization
  of Andes civilization, 39
  chiefdoms and, 32–33
  religion and, 41
  storage of goods and, 53
Poma, Huaman
  on Inca bureaucracy, 53
  on mines, 94
  on teenagers in Inca empire, 54
Popul Vuh, 68–69
Portuguese, 88–89, 93
Potosi (mine), 94
Poverty Point Culture, 9
Powhatan Wars (Virginia), 96
Pringle, Heather
  on Jacques Cinq-Mars, 15
Puche, Mari, 41
Pueblo Indians
  ancestors of, 28
  chiefdoms and, 33–34

Picture Credits

About the Author

Cathryn J. Long studied English literature at the University of California, Berkeley, where she earned a bachelor of arts degree and did graduate work. She has written a variety of books for students and others in the fields of history and world affairs. She is currently at work on a University of Cincinnati–sponsored project which allows people to visit prehistoric Indian earthworks and mounds through a computer-generated landscape.